C++ Programming Cookbook

Proven solutions using C++ 20 across functions, file I/O, streams, memory management, STL, concurrency, type manipulation and error debugging

Anais Sutherland

Published by: GitforGits

Publisher: Sonal Dhandre

www.gitforgits.com

support@gitforgits.com

Printed in India

First Printing: March 2024

ISBN: 9788119177622

Cover Design by: Kitten Publishing

Prologue

Let me tell you what this book is all about and why you should read it. My main objective has been to simplify the complex world of C++ into an engaging and informative set of instructional recipes. Whether you're just starting out in the world of programming or are an experienced developer looking to improve your C++ skills, I hope you'll find this cookbook to be a valuable learning based on my experiences, thoughts, and challenges.

The precision and strength of the C++ language make it ideal for developing a wide range of applications, from operating systems to game engines. Its expressiveness and adaptability have been enhanced via its evolution, particularly with the introduction of C++20 and further developments into C++23. By simplifying difficult ideas into actionable solutions that address actual issues, I hope to shed light on these developments in this book. With meticulous attention to detail, every chapter covers everything from the basics of variables and control structures to the complexities of concurrency, memory management, and everything in between, all of which are crucial for modern C++ development.

The greatest way to learn, in my opinion, is by doing, so I've taken a very practical approach. In-depth examples and exercises have been provided to show you how to use C++'s features and to make you think about the why and how of specific solutions. This book explores how to think creatively, solve problems analytically, and engage in continuous development. It is not just about C++ syntax.

My early days as a computer programmer were exciting and frustrating all at the same time. When my code finally ran as expected after compilation, I felt an overwhelming sense of accomplishment. But there were also many hours spent trying to figure out what was wrong and fix it. I learned the value of sticking with anything until you get it right, as well as the significance of knowing the language's fundamentals and the reasoning behind your own code, from these experiences. I hope to impart to you, through this book, this combination of technical expertise and perseverance.

It is important that you feel free to experiment, make mistakes, and ask questions as we explore into topics like as file I/O, stream operations, and the complexity of type manipulation. There is great joy in solving difficult issues with well-written, efficient code, and C++ is a language that encourages curiosity and hard labor. In addition to teaching you the technical abilities you'll need, this book aims to encourage an adventurous and creative spirit in its audience.

As we wrap up, I hope you'll come along for the ride as we delve into the world of modern C++. It is my sincere desire that this book serves as a dependable guide that you will consult often, whether you choose to read the chapters in order or delve into particular subjects that pique your interest. Every line of code is an opportunity to learn and grow with C++; the language is more like a journey than a destination. Come along with me as we explore the wonders of C++ programming with an open mind and a thirst for knowledge.

Content

Preface

"C++ Programming Cookbook" stands out as a clear, concise, and powerful technical resource for programmers who want to master C++'s intricacies. C++ programmers face a wide variety of problems, and this carefully written book is a treasure trove of solutions and methods to those software development challenges. Each chapter is organized to help you get a good grasp of the language and everything it can do, from the basics of C++20 to more complex topics like sophisticated type manipulation and performance optimization.

Through a series of carefully curated recipes, readers are invited on a journey of learning and competency. Starting with the fundamentals of creating a development environment and comprehending C++ syntax, the book progresses to cover more advanced subjects like concurrency, memory management, file I/O operations, object-oriented design concepts, functional programming, and more. This book focuses on the latest C++ features and aims to get programmers to use idiomatic C++ patterns and modern best practices.

"C++ Programming Cookbook" goes beyond being a mere collection of recipes; it serves as a manifesto for progressive software development practices and problem-solving. Readers are empowered to adapt and apply their learnings to new, unexplored situations because each recipe not only solves specific problems but also exposes fundamental ideas and methodologies. Writing code that is clean, efficient, and easy to maintain is a priority throughout the book, which aims to help readers develop a skill set that is applicable to more general programming problems.

With the goal of helping its readers become expert C++ programmers and problem solvers, this book is a must-have for anyone seeking to sharpen their programming skills. The "C++ Programming Cookbook" provides the information and insights needed to confidently and creatively navigate the always changing world of C++ programming, whether you're an experienced developer aiming for greatness or a newcomer ready to learn the ropes.

In this book you will learn how to:

- Make use of C++20 features to write more expressive, efficient, and modern C++ code effortlessly.
- Utilize template metaprogramming for compile-time calculations, enhancing code performance.
- Implement smart pointers for robust memory management without the usual complexity.
- Put object-oriented programming principles into use to design scalable and maintainable C++ applications.
- Explore advanced type manipulation techniques, ensuring type-safe and flexible code across applications.

- Harness concurrency and multithreading to build high-performance, responsive C++ software solutions.
- Optimize file I/O operations for seamless data handling in text and binary formats.
- Implement custom stream buffers for tailored data processing, boosting I/O efficiency.
- Navigate stream locales and facets for internationalizing your applications, reaching a global audience.
- Uncover efficient error and exception handling strategies to build reliable and error-free C++ programs.

GitforGits

Prerequisites

This book is for every programmer who is eager to or by no choice gets hooked up with C++ programming to code, build, improve and troubleshoot applications and systems. Prior knowledge of C++ version 11 and above is preferred to put every recipe into immediate use.

Codes Usage

Are you in need of some helpful code examples to assist you in your programming and documentation? Look no further! Our book offers a wealth of supplemental material, including code examples and exercises.

Not only is this book here to aid you in getting your job done, but you have our permission to use the example code in your programs and documentation. However, please note that if you are reproducing a significant portion of the code, we do require you to contact us for permission.

But don't worry, using several chunks of code from this book in your program or answering a question by citing our book and quoting example code does not require permission. But if you do choose to give credit, an attribution typically includes the title, author, publisher, and ISBN. For example, "C++ Programming Cookbook by Anais Sutherland".

If you are unsure whether your intended use of the code examples falls under fair use or the permissions outlined above, please do not hesitate to reach out to us at support@gitforgits.com.

We are happy to assist and clarify any concerns.

Acknowledgement

I owe a tremendous debt of gratitude to GitforGits, for their unflagging enthusiasm and wise counsel throughout the entire process of writing this book. Their knowledge and careful editing helped make sure the piece was useful for people of all reading levels and comprehension skills. In addition, I'd like to thank everyone involved in the publishing process for their efforts in making this book a reality. Their efforts, from copyediting to advertising, made the project what it is today.

Finally, I'd like to express my gratitude to everyone who has shown me unconditional love and encouragement throughout my life. Their support was crucial to the completion of this book. I appreciate your help with this endeavour and your continued interest in my career.

CHAPTER 1: GETTING STARTED WITH C++20

Introduction

Welcome to the exciting world of modern C++ programming! Chapter 1, "Getting Started with C++20," will cover all the basics. This fundamental chapter attempts to provide you with the key tools, knowledge, and abilities needed to negotiate the complexities of C++20, laying the groundwork for more advanced topics covered in subsequent chapters. We begin by leading you through the process of creating a C++20-specific development environment, ensuring that you have the necessary compiler and tools to take use of all of C++20's capabilities.

Understanding C++'s core grammar and program structure is critical, and we will go over those topics to ensure you are comfortable creating clear and precise C++. From variables, data types, and type deduction to control structures such as if-else, switch, and loops, you'll learn how to navigate the language's fundamental building blocks with confidence.

We will also go over functions in depth, including basics, overloading, and default arguments, so you can develop diverse and powerful code. Namespaces and the preprocessor will be emphasized as important tools for organizing code and properly managing compilation processes. Finally, understanding fundamental input and output is critical for any program, and we will guarantee you are comfortable engaging with users and processing data efficiently.

By the end of this chapter, you'll have a thorough understanding of C++20's key concepts and be ready to take on increasingly complicated programming challenges with confidence.

Recipe 1: Setting Up the C++20 Development Environment

Situation

Before entering into the complexities of C++20 programming, you must have a development environment that fully supports the new features and improvements included in this version. For Windows users, this entails selecting the appropriate compiler and development tools that are current and compliant with C++20 standards.

Practical Solution

To start programming with C++20 on Windows, the most straightforward approach is to use Microsoft's Visual Studio, one of the most popular and powerful IDEs (Integrated Development Environments) for C++ development. Visual Studio 2019 and later versions offer comprehensive support for C++20 features.

Given below is how to set it up:

Download and Install Visual Studio

Visit the official Microsoft Visual Studio website to download the Visual Studio installer. The Community Edition is free for students, open-source contributors, and individuals. During installation, select the "Desktop development with C++" workload, which includes the necessary C++ compilers and libraries for desktop application development.

Configure Your Project for C++20

Once installed, launch Visual Studio and create a new project. Choose a template that suits your needs, such as a "Console App." After creating your project, you'll need to configure it to use the C++20 standard. Right-click on your project in the Solution Explorer, select "Properties," navigate to "Configuration Properties" > "C/C++" > "Language," and then set the "C++ Language Standard" option to "ISO C++20 Standard (/std:c++20)."

Verify Your Setup

To ensure everything is set up correctly, we must write a simple program that utilizes a C++20 feature, such as the **constexpr** with virtual functions. Create a new **.cpp** file in your project and add the following code:

```
#include <iostream>


struct Base {

 virtual constexpr int getValue() { return 5; }

};


struct Derived : Base {

 constexpr int getValue() override { return 10; }

};


int main() {
```

```
constexpr Derived d;

static_assert(d.getValue() == 10, "The value must be 10");

std::cout << "C++20 is configured correctly!\n";

return 0;

}
```

Build and Run Your Project

After writing the code, build your project by selecting "Build" from the menu and then "Build Solution." If everything is configured correctly, there should be no errors, and you can run your application by pressing F5 or clicking the "Start Debugging" button. The output should confirm that C++20 is set up correctly in your development environment.

Following these steps will result in a rich development environment on Windows that is specifically designed for learning about and employing the full capabilities of C++20, opening the way for future recipes that delve into more sophisticated programming concepts and features.

Recipe 2: Basic Syntax and Program Structure

Situation

After setting up your C++20 development environment, the next step is to understand the basic syntax and structure of a C++ program. This knowledge forms the foundation of your coding experience, enabling you to write clear, efficient, and error-free code.

Practical Solution

A standard C++ program consists of one or more functions, with **main()** being the entry point of the application. The structure of a C++ program includes preprocessor directives, function definitions, and, optionally, global variables, classes, and more. We shall break down these components with a simple example that illustrates the fundamental syntax and structure of a C++ program.

Preprocessor Directives

These are instructions that are processed before the actual compilation of code begins. They typically include file inclusion or macro definitions. The **#include** directive is used to include the contents of a standard library or user-defined header files.

main() Function

Every C++ program must have a **main()** function. This is the entry point from where execution starts. The **main()** function can return an integer and take arguments, although for simple programs, these arguments are often omitted.

Statements and Expressions

Inside functions, you'll write statements and expressions that define the specific instructions to be executed. Statements end with a semicolon (;).

Comments

Comments are used for adding explanatory notes to the code and are ignored by the compiler. Single-line comments start with **//**, while multi-line comments are enclosed between **/*** and ***/**.

Simple C++ Program "Welcome to GitforGits!"

We shall put this together in a simple C++ program that prints "Welcome to GitforGits!" to the console:

```
#include <iostream> // Includes the Standard Library's input/output stream


// The main() function - starting point of the program

int main() {

 // Outputs "Welcome to GitforGits!" to the console

 std::cout << "Welcome to GitforGits!" << std::endl; // Uses std::cout for output,
followed by the insertion operator (<<)


 return 0; // Successful program termination signal

}
```

In this revised example:

#include <iostream> is a directive that includes the I/O stream library, necessary for output operations.

The **int main()** function marks the program's entry, returning an integer to indicate execution success.

std::cout << "Welcome to GitforGits!" << std::endl; outputs our welcome message to the console, followed by an end-of-line marker (**std::endl**), ensuring the console cursor moves to the next line.

The program concludes with **return 0;**, indicating successful execution.

This program, "Welcome to GitforGits!", will now serve as our starting point as we explore deeper into the principles in this chapter. To build any C++ application, you must master this fundamental structure and syntax. Only then can you take on more complex programming problems.

Recipe 3: Variables, Data Types, and Type Deduction

Situation

Considering that you've got a grasp on the basic syntax and structure of a C++ program, it's time to dive deeper into the core components that make up the logic of any application: variables, data types, and type deduction. These elements are crucial for storing information and manipulating data in your programs.

Practical Solution

In C++, variables are containers for storing data values. Each variable has a data type that determines the size and layout of the variable's memory; the range of values that can be stored within that memory; and the set of operations that can be applied to the variable.

Variables and Data Types

The basic data types in C++ include **int** for integers, **double** for floating-point numbers, **char** for characters, and **bool** for boolean values (true/false). We shall enhance our "Welcome to GitforGits!" program to use some variables:

```
#include <iostream>


int main() {

 int year = 2024; // An integer variable to store the year
```

```
double version = 20.0; // A double variable for C++ version
char initial = 'G'; // A character variable for initial letter
bool isUpdated = true; // A boolean variable to indicate update status

std::cout << "Welcome to GitforGits!" << std::endl;
std::cout << "Year: " << year << ", C++ Version: " << version << std::endl;
std::cout << "Initial: " << initial << ", Updated: " << isUpdated << std::endl;

return 0;
}
```

Type Deduction with auto

C++11 introduced **auto**, which instructs the compiler to automatically deduce the type of a variable from its initializer. The use of **auto** can simplify the code and make it more readable, especially when dealing with complex types. C++20 continues to support and encourage the use of **auto** for type deduction. Given below is how you can use **auto** in our example:

```
#include <iostream>

int main() {
auto year = 2024; // The compiler deduces that year is an int
auto version = 20.0; // version is deduced to be double
auto initial = 'G'; // initial is deduced to be char
auto isUpdated = true; // isUpdated is deduced to be bool
```

```
std::cout << "Welcome to GitforGits!" << std::endl;

std::cout << "Year: " << year << ", C++ Version: " << version << std::endl;

std::cout << "Initial: " << initial << ", Updated: " << isUpdated << std::endl;


return 0;

}
```

By using **auto**, we let the compiler figure out the type based on the value assigned to the variable, which can significantly reduce the verbosity of the code, especially with more complex data types or when using templates and iterators.

In this recipe, we've seen how to declare variables, understand basic data types, and leverage type deduction with **auto** to make our code cleaner and more maintainable.

Recipe 4: If-Else, Switch, and Loops

Situation

As you continue to develop your programming skills with C++20, understanding control flow mechanisms is essential. These include conditional statements like **if-else** and **switch**, as well as loops like **for**, **while**, and **do-while**, which control the execution path of your program based on conditions and iterations. Integrating these constructs into our ongoing "Welcome to GitforGits!" example will demonstrate your practical use in real-world scenarios.

Practical Solution

If-Else Statements

These are used to execute code blocks based on a condition. If the condition evaluates to true, the first block of code executes; if false, the code in the else block executes.

```
#include <iostream>
```

```
int main() {
 auto year = 2024;
 // Check if the current year is 2024 or not
 if (year == 2024) {
 std::cout << "Welcome to GitforGits in 2024!" << std::endl;
 } else {
 std::cout << "Welcome to GitforGits in another year!" << std::endl;
 }
 // Proceed with the rest of the program...
}
```

Switch Statements

A **switch** statement allows you to choose from multiple options based on an expression's value. It's a cleaner alternative to multiple **if-else** statements when dealing with variable conditions.

```
auto version = 20; // Assuming version is an integer
switch (version) {
 case 20:
 std::cout << "You're using C++20." << std::endl;
 break;
 case 17:
 std::cout << "You're using C++17." << std::endl;
 break;
```

```
default:
std::cout << "Unknown C++ version." << std::endl;
}
```

Loops

Loops are used to execute a block of code repeatedly based on a condition. C++ provides **for**, **while**, and **do-while** loops.

- For Loop: Ideal for iterating a known number of times.

```
for (int i = 1; i <= 5; i++) {
std::cout << "Iteration " << i << std::endl;
}
```

- While Loop: Executes as long as a condition remains true. Useful when the number of iterations isn't known before the loop starts.

```
int i = 1;
while (i <= 5) {
std::cout << "Iteration " << i << std::endl;
i++;
}
```

- Do-While Loop: Similar to the **while** loop, but the condition is evaluated after the execution of the loop's body, ensuring that the body is executed at least once.

```
int i = 1;
do {
std::cout << "Iteration " << i << std::endl;
```

```
i++;

} while (i <= 5);
```

You may make your C++ applications more flexible and robust by including these control flow technologies. They allow for dynamic execution pathways and repeating actions.

Recipe 5: Basics, Overloading, and Default Arguments

Situation

Functions are fundamental in structuring and organizing C++ programs into logical blocks of code. As we advance our chapter with the "Welcome to GitforGits!" application, understanding how to define, use, overload functions, and employ default arguments becomes crucial. These concepts not only enhance modularity but also improve code readability and reusability.

Practical Solution

Function Basics

In C++, a function is a group of statements that perform a specific task. Every C++ program has at least one function, **main()**, and can have additional user-defined functions. Given below is a basic function structure:

```
// Function declaration

returnType functionName(parameterList);


// Function definition

returnType functionName(parameterList) {

 // function body

}
```

We shall add a simple function to our program that greets the user:

```
#include <iostream>


// Function declaration

void greetUser();


int main() {

 greetUser();

 return 0;

}


// Function definition

void greetUser() {

 std::cout << "Welcome to GitforGits!" << std::endl;

}
```

This **greetUser** function, when called, prints a greeting message. The **void** return type indicates that it does not return a value.

Function Overloading

Function overloading allows multiple functions to have the same name with different parameters (different type or number of parameters). It enables functions to perform similar operations on different data types.

```
#include <iostream>
```

```
// Overloaded functions
void display(int i) {
 std::cout << "Displaying int: " << i << std::endl;
}

void display(double d) {
 std::cout << "Displaying double: " << d << std::endl;
}

void display(std::string s) {
 std::cout << "Displaying string: " << s << std::endl;
}

int main() {
 display(10); // Calls display(int)
 display(10.5); // Calls display(double)
 display(GitforGits); // Calls display(std::string)
 return 0;
}
```

In the above code snippet, the **display** function is overloaded to handle **int**, **double**, and **std::string** types, showcasing polymorphism.

Default Arguments

Default arguments in functions allow you to call a function with fewer arguments than it is defined to accept. The default values are used for any parameters that are omitted.

```
#include <iostream>


// Function with default argument
void logMessage(std::string message = "Default log message") {
 std::cout << message << std::endl;
}


int main() {
 logMessage("Welcome to GitforGits!"); // Uses provided argument
 logMessage(); // Uses default argument
 return 0;
}
```

This function, **logMessage**, can be called either with a custom message or without any arguments, in which case the default message is used. This feature enhances function flexibility and simplifies calls for common use cases.

Incorporating in "Welcome to GitforGits!" Program

How about we update our "Welcome to GitforGits!" software with a function that shows the current version? We can use overloading to accept numerical or textual version identifiers, and for typical cases, we can use a default argument:

```
#include <iostream>
```

```
// Function declarations
void displayVersion(int version);
void displayVersion(std::string versionDetail);
void greetUser(std::string name = "Guest");

int main() {
 displayVersion(20); // Display numerical version
 displayVersion("Version 20.0 - Stable"); // Display version detail
 greetUser(); // Greet a guest user
 greetUser("Alice"); // Greet a specific user
 return 0;
}

// Display version number
void displayVersion(int version) {
 std::cout << "GitforGits C++ Version: " << version << std::endl;
}

// Display version detail
void displayVersion(std::string versionDetail) {
 std::cout << "GitforGits " << versionDetail << std::endl;
```

```
}

// Greet user with optional name
void greetUser(std::string name) {
 std::cout << "Welcome to GitforGits, " << name << "!" << std::endl;
}
```

In this enhanced version, **displayVersion** is overloaded to accept either an integer or a string, allowing for flexible display options. Additionally, **greetUser** includes a default argument, making it versatile for situations where the user's name might not be provided.

This recipe has covered the principles of constructing and utilizing functions, the power of overloading for polymorphism, and the convenience of default arguments to enable flexibility in function calls. As we expand on our "Welcome to GitforGits!" example, these fundamental principles of C++ programming will allow us to handle increasingly sophisticated logic and functionality with ease.

Recipe 6: Namespaces and the Preprocessor

Situation

As the "Welcome to GitforGits!" application grows in complexity, organizing your code becomes increasingly important to ensure clarity and avoid naming conflicts. This is where namespaces and preprocessor directives come into play. Namespaces allow you to group logically related entities, such as functions and classes, under a named scope, preventing naming collisions. Preprocessor directives, on the other hand, offer a way to include files, define macros, and conditionally compile parts of your program, among other things. Understanding these concepts is crucial for managing large codebases and making your code more modular and maintainable.

Practical Solution

Using Namespaces

Namespaces prevent naming conflicts by enclosing identifiers in a named scope. The **std** namespace, for example, contains all the standard C++ library names. To create and use your own namespace for the "Welcome to GitforGits!" project, follow this approach:

```
#include <iostream>


namespace gitforgits {

 void greet() {

 std::cout << "Welcome to GitforGits!" << std::endl;

 }

 // Further functions and classes related to GitforGits can be added here

}


int main() {

 // Accessing the greet function within the gitforgits namespace

 gitforgits::greet();

 return 0;

}
```

Using **namespace gitforgits**, we encapsulate the **greet** function within our own custom scope. This method prevents potential naming conflicts with other libraries or parts of the program.

Exploring Preprocessor Directives

Preprocessor directives are lines included in your code that are not part of the C++ language itself but are instructions for the preprocessor. These directives can include header files, define constants, or conditionally compile parts of the code.

- Including Header Files: The **#include** directive is used to include the contents of a file in the program. This is commonly used to include standard library headers or your own header files for class definitions.

- Defining Macros: The **#define** directive allows you to define macros, which are snippets of code that are given a name. When the name is used in the code, it's replaced by the code snippet.
- Conditional Compilation: The **#ifdef**, **#ifndef**, **#endif**, **#if**, and **#else** directives let you compile parts of the code conditionally. This can be useful for debugging or compiling code for different platforms.

Following is an example that demonstrates the use of preprocessor directives within our project:

```
#include <iostream>

#define WELCOME_MESSAGE "Welcome to GitforGits!"


int main() {

 std::cout << WELCOME_MESSAGE << std::endl;

 return 0;

}
```

In the above code snippet, **#define WELCOME_MESSAGE "Welcome to GitforGits!"** creates a macro for the welcome message, making the code more readable and easier to update.

Recipe 7: Exceptions and Assertions

Situation

In any robust application, like "Welcome to GitforGits!", handling unexpected situations gracefully is crucial for maintaining data integrity and providing a seamless user experience. C++ offers two primary mechanisms for error handling and debugging: exceptions and assertions. Exceptions provide a way to react to exceptional circumstances (like runtime errors) that occur during program execution, while assertions are used to check for conditions that must always be true unless there's a bug in the program. Understanding how to effectively use these tools is essential for building resilient and reliable software.

Practical Solution

Understanding and Using Exceptions

Exceptions in C++ are a powerful mechanism for handling runtime errors. They allow a program to transfer control from one part of the code to another when an error occurs, making your code cleaner and more readable.

To use exceptions, you'll typically follow these steps:

- Throw an exception using the **throw** keyword when a problem is detected.
- Catch the exception with a **try-catch** block where you can handle the error gracefully.

We shall apply exceptions to our "Welcome to GitforGits!" application by adding a function that checks the version of the program and throws an exception if the version is not supported:

```
#include <iostream>

#include <stdexcept> // Include for std::runtime_error


void checkVersion(int version) {

 if (version < 20) {

 throw std::runtime_error("This version of GitforGits is not supported.");

 }

 std::cout << "You are using GitforGits version " << version << std::endl;

}


int main() {

 try {

 checkVersion(19); // Try with an unsupported version

 } catch (const std::runtime_error& e) {

 std::cerr << "Error: " << e.what() << std::endl;
```

```
// Handle error or exit

return 1; // Indicate failure

}

return 0; // Indicate success

}
```

In the above given code snippet, **checkVersion** throws a **std::runtime_error** if the version is below 20. The **main** function catches this exception and prints an error message, demonstrating how exceptions can be used for error handling.

Leveraging Assertions for Debugging

Assertions are a debugging aid that checks for boolean conditions that should be true during the execution of a program. If an assertion fails (the condition evaluates to **false**), the program will terminate with an error message. Assertions are implemented with the **assert** macro from the **<cassert>** header and are typically used to catch programming errors during the development phase.

Given below is how you might use an assertion in the "Welcome to GitforGits!" project:

```
#include <iostream>

#include <cassert>


void printVersion(int version) {

assert(version > 0 && "Version must be positive"); // The program will terminate if version is not positive

std::cout << "GitforGits version " << version << std::endl;

}


int main() {
```

```
printVersion(20); // Correct usage

//printVersion(-1); // Uncommenting this line will cause the assertion to fail

return 0;

}
```

In the above given code snippet, the **assert** statement checks that the version is positive. If you uncomment the call to **printVersion(-1)**, the assertion will fail, and the program will terminate, indicating a bug that needs to be fixed. Exceptions allow for robust error handling in situations where operations may fail at runtime, enabling your programs to recover gracefully from unexpected events. Assertions, on the other hand, are used to ensure that certain conditions always hold true, serving as a safeguard against programming errors.

Recipe 8: Basic Input and Output

Situation

Effective communication with the user is a cornerstone of interactive applications. In our journey with "Welcome to GitforGits!", incorporating user feedback and providing meaningful output is crucial for a dynamic user experience. C++ facilitates this interaction through its standard input and output (I/O) streams, allowing you to receive input from the user (via the keyboard) and display output (to the console). Grasping these basic I/O operations is essential for developing interactive applications.

Practical Solution

Standard Output with std::cout

In C++, **std::cout** is used for sending output to the console. It's part of the iostream library, which provides facilities for input and output operations. Given below is how you might use **std::cout** to display a welcome message and version information in "Welcome to GitforGits!":

```
#include <iostream>



int main() {
```

```
int version = 20;

std::cout << "Welcome to GitforGits!" << std::endl;

std::cout << "You are using version " << version << std::endl;

return 0;

}
```

std::endl is used here not only to insert a newline character but also to flush the output buffer, ensuring that the output is immediately displayed to the user.

Standard Input with std::cin

std::cin is used for reading input from the user. Together with **std::cout**, it forms the basis of console I/O in C++. We shall enhance our program to prompt the user for their name and customize the greeting message:

```
#include <iostream>

#include <string> // Include for std::string


int main() {

std::string userName;

std::cout << "Please enter your name: ";

std::cin >> userName; // Reads input from the console and stores it in userName

std::cout << "Welcome to GitforGits, " << userName << "!" << std::endl;

return 0;

}
```

When using **std::cin** to read input, it's important to be aware of its behavior with different data types and how it handles whitespace and newline characters. For instance, **std::cin >>**

userName; will read input until the first whitespace character is encountered.

Combining Input and Output for Interactive Apps

By combining **std::cin** and **std::cout**, you can create more interactive and user-friendly console applications. Given below is a simple example where the user is asked to enter the current year, and the program checks if it matches the version year of "Welcome to GitforGits!":

```
#include <iostream>


int main() {

 int currentYear, versionYear = 2024;

 std::cout << "Enter the current year: ";

 std::cin >> currentYear;


 if (currentYear == versionYear) {

 std::cout << "You are up to date with GitforGits!" << std::endl;

 } else {

 std::cout << "It's time to update your GitforGits!" << std::endl;

 }

 return 0;

}
```

Through **std::cout** and **std::cin**, you can display information to the user and receive their input, respectively. As you progress with "Welcome to GitforGits!", experimenting with these I/O operations will significantly enhance your ability to engage users and respond to their input dynamically.

Summary

Chapter 1 of our C++20 adventure with the "Welcome to GitforGits!" project covered the basics of current C++ programming with an emphasis on practical, hands-on learning. We began by setting up a C++20-specific development environment before moving on to the fundamentals of grammar and program structure, emphasizing the significance of developing clear and efficient code. We looked at variables, data types, and the power of type deduction with auto, demonstrating how to manage data successfully in our apps. Functions, a key component of organized code, were deconstructed to better understand their declaration, definition, overloading capabilities, and use of default arguments, all of which improve the modularity and readability of our code.

Using control flow methods including as if-else statements, switch cases, and loops, we learnt to dynamically influence the execution flow of our programs in response to conditions and iterations. The introduction of namespaces and preprocessor directives provided us with tools for structuring code and managing compilation processes, assuring clarity and avoiding naming conflicts. Exception handling and assertions were identified as critical strategies for reliable error handling and debugging, guaranteeing that our programs recover gracefully from unforeseen situations and are free of logical mistakes.

Finally, the critical topic of engaging with the user via fundamental input and output activities was discussed, emphasizing the value of interactive apps. We made it easier to create user-friendly interfaces by mastering std::cout for output and std::cin for input. Each recipe builds on the previous one, resulting in a thorough mastery of the principles required for advancement in C++ programming. This chapter not only laid the groundwork for more advanced concepts, but it also assured that we have the practical skills to begin developing useful and efficient C++20 programs.

CHAPTER 2: DEEP DIVE INTO FUNCTIONS

Introduction

The second chapter, "Deep Dive into Functions," explores deeply into the flexibility and strength of C++20 functions. This chapter is designed to help you understand how functions can be optimized, altered, and used to produce more efficient and understandable code. Through a series of focused recipes, we will explore the complexities of inline and constexpr functions, demonstrating how they improve efficiency by reducing function call overhead and allowing compile-time evaluation.

Lambda expressions, a feature that has considerably simplified how functions are used and defined, particularly in the context of algorithms and event handlers, will be examined to better grasp their syntax, capture modes, and practical uses. The subject will go on to function pointers and functors, where they will be explained in relation to callback systems and object-oriented function calls. We will also go into the subtleties of using templates within functions to promote code reuse and flexibility across various data types.

The research continues with a review of C++'s wide range of standard library functions and algorithms, with a focus on how to use them efficiently to accomplish typical programming tasks and manage data structures. In addition, the chapter will teach specialized error handling in functions to create strong and reliable software. Function overloading and name mangling will be explained in detail, with a focus on how C++ distinguishes between different versions of overloaded functions. Finally, we will look at how to strategically employ the auto keyword within functions to simplify code and make it more maintainable. This chapter promises to provide you with a thorough understanding of function implementation and utilization, hence improving your coding productivity and the quality of your C++ applications.

Recipe 1: Exploring Inline and Constexpr Functions

Situation

As we dive into the depths of C++20, optimizing function performance and ensuring compile-time evaluation where possible are key to writing efficient code. This is particularly important in resource-constrained environments or when processing speed is critical. Two powerful tools at our disposal are inline and constexpr functions. Inline functions are a hint to the compiler to attempt to embed the function's body wherever it's called, reducing the overhead of a function call. On the other hand, constexpr functions enable certain computations to occur at compile time, saving runtime resources and ensuring constants are truly constant throughout the application.

Practical Solution

Inline Functions

Traditionally, the **inline** keyword suggests to the compiler that it should attempt to embed the function directly into the calling code, rather than performing a standard function call. This can lead to performance improvements, especially in short, frequently called functions. However, the compiler is not obliged to inline your function; it's merely a suggestion that the compiler can ignore based on its optimization rules.

Given below is a simple example of an inline function:

```
inline int add(int a, int b) {
 return a + b;
}

int main() {
 int result = add(5, 3);
 std::cout << "The sum is: " << result << std::endl;
 return 0;
}
```

Constexpr Functions

Constexpr functions are executed at compile time when called with constexpr arguments, enabling compile-time computations and ensuring the results are available during compilation. This is incredibly useful for defining constants that are computed but remain constant throughout the application's execution.

An example of a constexpr function might look like this:

```
constexpr int factorial(int n) {
 return (n <= 1) ? 1 : (n * factorial(n - 1));
}
```

```
int main() {
 constexpr int result = factorial(5); // Compute at compile time
 std::cout << "The factorial of 5 is: " << result << std::endl;
 return 0;
}
```

In this case, **factorial(5)** is evaluated at compile time, and its result, **120**, is used as a compile-time constant within the program.

Recipe 2: Using Lambda Expressions

Situation

In modern C++ programming, lambda expressions have become a pivotal feature for writing concise and functional-style code, especially when dealing with algorithms that require custom operations or when working with event-driven programming models. Lambdas allow you to define anonymous functions directly within the context they are used, making your code more readable and expressive. Understanding how to effectively use lambda expressions can significantly benefit your learnings from this chapter, enhancing the flexibility and maintainability of your applications.

Practical Solution

What Are Lambda Expressions?

A lambda expression in C++ can be thought of as a concise way to write an inline function that can be used for short snippets of code that are not going to be reused elsewhere. It's particularly useful for passing as an argument to functions, especially those that take function pointers or functors, like many of the standard library algorithms.

Syntax and Functionality

The basic syntax of a lambda expression looks like this:

```
[ capture_clause ] ( parameters ) -> return_type {
```

```
// function body
}
```

- Capture Clause: Specifies which variables from the enclosing scope are available inside the lambda, and whether they are captured by value or by reference.
- Parameters: Like regular functions, you can pass parameters to a lambda.
- Return Type: Optionally, you can explicitly specify a return type. If omitted, it's inferred from the return statements in the lambda's body.
- Function Body: The code block that defines what the lambda does.

Benefits for Applications

Lambda expressions can make your code more straightforward by reducing the need for named functions, especially for simple operations that are used only once. They're also incredibly powerful when used with the standard library's algorithms or for setting up callbacks in event-driven or GUI applications.

Let us consider that we want to sort a vector of integers in descending order using the **std::sort** algorithm from the C++ standard library. A lambda expression makes this task easy and expressive:

```
#include <vector>
#include <algorithm>
#include <iostream>

int main() {
 std::vector<int> numbers{4, 1, 3, 5, 2};
 // Sort in descending order using a lambda expression
 std::sort(numbers.begin(), numbers.end(), [](int a, int b) {
 return a > b; // Specify the sort criteria directly
```

```
});

// Print the sorted vector
for (int n : numbers) {
std::cout << n << ' ';
}
std::cout << '\n';

return 0;
}
```

In the above given sample program, the lambda expression **[](int a, int b) { return a > b; }** defines an anonymous function that the **std::sort** algorithm uses to compare elements. This simple expression, which appears directly within the sort function call, highlights lambda expressions' power and versatility in simplifying and expressing code. You may improve the expressiveness and speed of your code by incorporating lambdas into your applications, particularly when working with standard library algorithms, callbacks, or any situation that requires simple, on-the-spot functions.

Recipe 3: Exploring Function Pointers and Functors

Situation

Moving deeper into the functionalities of C++20 and its application in various programming paradigms, understanding the concept of function pointers and functors opens up a new dimension of passing behavior as parameters, enabling higher-order functions. Function pointers allow you to store the address of a function in a variable, facilitating dynamic function invocation. Functors, on the other hand, are objects that can be treated as though they are a function or function pointer. Both concepts are invaluable in scenarios where you need to pass around and execute functions dynamically, such as in callback mechanisms or when using algorithms that require custom operations.

Practical Solution

Function Pointers

Function pointers hold the address of a function, allowing the function to be called through the pointer. They are particularly useful for callback functions and for implementing polymorphism in C programs.

Given below is a simple example of using a function pointer:

```
#include <iostream>


void greet() {

 std::cout << "Hello from greet function." << std::endl;

}


int main() {

 void (*funcPtr)() = greet; // Declaring a function pointer and assigning it to greet

 funcPtr(); // Calling the function through the pointer

 return 0;

}
```

In the above given sample program, **funcPtr** is a pointer to a function that takes no parameters and returns nothing (**void**). It is assigned the address of the **greet** function and then used to call **greet**.

Functors (Function Objects)

Functors are objects that can be called as if they were ordinary functions based on the operator overloading of the function call operator **()**. This makes them more flexible than function pointers since they can also hold state.

Given below is how you can define and use a functor:

```
#include <iostream>


class GreetFunctor {
public:
 void operator()() const {
 std::cout << "Hello from GreetFunctor." << std::endl;
 }
};


int main() {
 GreetFunctor greet;
 greet(); // Using the functor to call the function
 return 0;
}
```

The **GreetFunctor** class defines the function call operator **operator()**, which allows objects of **GreetFunctor** to be used as if they were functions.

For advanced C++ programming, it is essential to understand these principles, whether you choose function pointers for your simplicity and directness or functors for your capacity to encapsulate state and behavior. When it comes to building algorithms, callbacks, and event-driven programs, your strong methods of abstracting and passing around behavior are invaluable.

Recipe 4: Templates within Functions

Situation

As we venture further into the intricacies of C++20, templates emerge as a pivotal feature enabling generic programming. By allowing functions to operate on data of various types without being rewritten for each type, templates dramatically enhance code reusability and flexibility. This concept is especially beneficial in creating libraries or utilities where operations need to be generalized across different data types. Understanding how to effectively implement templates within functions can significantly elevate your programming prowess, making your applications more scalable and maintainable.

Practical Solution

Function Templates

Function templates are a way to write a single function that can operate on different data types. The compiler automatically generates the appropriate function definition when the template is instantiated with a specific type. This eliminates the need for multiple function overloads, each handling a different data type.

Given below is a simple program of a function template:

```
#include <iostream>


// Template function to add two values

template <typename T>

T add(T a, T b) {

 return a + b;

}


int main() {

 std::cout << add<int>(5, 3) << std::endl; // Instantiates and calls add for int
```

```
 std::cout << add<double>(2.5, 3.5) << std::endl; // Instantiates and calls add for double

 std::cout << add<std::string>("Git", "forGits") << std::endl; // Instantiates and calls add for std::string



 return 0;

}
```

In the above given sample program, the **add** function is defined once using a template, but it can add integers, doubles, and even concatenate strings, depending on the types it's instantiated with.

Advantages of Templates

- Unlike using void pointers or other generic techniques, templates provide type safety without sacrificing performance, as the type checking happens at compile time.
- Write your algorithm once and use it for any data type, reducing code duplication.
- Since the compiler generates the code for the specific type, template-based code can be as fast as code written specifically for that type.

Tips for Function Templates

- In C++14 and later, you can use **auto** as the return type of template functions to make the syntax cleaner, especially when the return type is complex or depends on the template parameters.
- With C++20, you can use concepts to specify constraints on the template parameters, ensuring that the function template is only instantiated with types that meet certain requirements.

Recipe 5: Standard Library Functions and Algorithms

Situation

The C++ Standard Library is a powerful set of pre-written classes and functions designed to be reusable across many programs. Within this library, a significant portion is dedicated to functions and algorithms that operate on containers, like arrays, lists, and vectors. These algorithms include operations for sorting, searching, counting, transforming data, and much more. Leveraging these standard library functions and algorithms not only saves development time but also ensures that your code is efficient, reliable, and well-tested. For anyone diving deep into C++ functions, understanding and utilizing these tools is essential for writing sophisticated and high-performance applications.

Practical Solution

Exploring Key Functions and Algorithms

The C++ Standard Library includes a variety of algorithms that work with iterators, making them applicable to any container type. Following are some commonly used algorithms and how they can be applied:

- Sorting: **std::sort(begin, end)** sorts the elements between two iterators. It's one of the most frequently used algorithms and is highly optimized for performance.
- Searching: **std::find(begin, end, value)** searches for a value within a container and returns an iterator to the first matching element, if found.
- Counting: **std::count(begin, end, value)** counts the occurrences of a specific value within a container.
- Transforming: **std::transform(begin, end, destination, unary_operation)** applies a function to a range of elements, storing the result in a destination range.

We shall enhance our ongoing project with some standard library algorithms to process a list of version numbers:

```
#include <iostream>

#include <vector>

#include <algorithm>



int main() {

 std::vector<int> versions{20, 17, 20, 15, 20};
```

```
// Sort the versions
std::sort(versions.begin(), versions.end());

// Find a specific version
auto it = std::find(versions.begin(), versions.end(), 17);
if (it != versions.end()) {
std::cout << "Version 17 found." << std::endl;
}

// Count occurrences of version 20
int count20 = std::count(versions.begin(), versions.end(), 20);
std::cout << "Version 20 appears " << count20 << " times." << std::endl;

// Increment all versions by 1 using std::transform
std::transform(versions.begin(), versions.end(), versions.begin(), [](int v) { return ++v;
});

std::cout << "Updated versions: ";
for (int v : versions) {
std::cout << v << " ";
}
std::cout << std::endl;
```

```
return 0;

}
```

Instead of worrying about making everything from scratch, you can concentrate on making your application special by incorporating these industry-standard solutions. The Standard Library contains well-optimized and user-friendly interfaces for sorting data, searching for elements, and modifying collections, which can considerably improve the usefulness and efficiency of your C++ programs.

Recipe 6: Custom Error Handling in Functions

Situation

In the development of complex applications like "Welcome to GitforGits," robust error handling becomes a cornerstone for creating reliable and user-friendly software. The ability to gracefully manage and respond to errors not only enhances the application's resilience but also improves the overall user experience by providing clear feedback and avoiding unexpected crashes. Building on our exploration of C++ functionalities, this recipe delves into custom error handling within functions, offering a structured approach to anticipate, catch, and manage potential issues that may arise during execution.

Practical Solution

To incorporate custom error handling into our application, we can define our own exception classes, throw exceptions in scenarios where errors occur, and catch these exceptions to provide meaningful responses.

Defining Custom Exception Classes

Creating a custom exception class allows you to tailor error messages and categorize errors more precisely.

```
#include <exception>

#include <string>
```

```
class VersionException : public std::exception {

private:

 std::string message;

public:

 VersionException(const std::string& msg) : message(msg) {}


 // Override what() to provide the custom error message

 virtual const char* what() const throw() {

 return message.c_str();

 }

};
```

Throwing Exceptions in Functions

Within our application functions, we can throw exceptions when we encounter an error condition. For example, consider adding a function to check if the application version meets a minimum requirement and throw a **VersionException** if it does not:

```
void checkVersionCompatibility(int currentVersion) {

 const int minimumVersion = 20;

 if (currentVersion < minimumVersion) {

 throw VersionException("GitforGits version is outdated. Please update to the latest version.");

 }

}
```

Catching and Handling Exceptions

When using functions that may throw exceptions, surround the calls with a try-catch block to handle potential errors gracefully.

```
int main() {
 try {
 checkVersionCompatibility(15); // This will throw an exception
 } catch (const VersionException& e) {
 std::cerr << "Error: " << e.what() << std::endl;
 // Additional error handling logic can go here
 return 1; // Exit the program or take corrective action
 }
 std::cout << "Version is compatible." << std::endl;
 return 0;
}
```

This technique showcases the best practices in software development, which include improving the dependability of the application and preparing for any faults as much as developing the essential capabilities.

Recipe 7: Function Overloading and Name Mangling

Situation

You'll find times when you need more than one function with the same name but different arguments as you learn more about how your application works. This is known as function overloading, and it is a key component of polymorphism in C++. Overloading allows functions to be adapted to the context of their call, resulting in greater flexibility and clarity in how they are utilized. However, this introduces the concept of name mangling (or name decorating), which is how the C++ compiler distinguishes between overloaded functions during the linking process.

Practical Solution

Function Overloading

Overloading allows multiple functions to have the same name with different parameters. It enables you to use the same function name for different types or operations, improving code readability and usability.

Following is an example of overloading within our application, offering different greetings based on the time of day:

```
#include <iostream>

#include <string>


void greet() {

 std::cout << "Welcome to GitforGits!" << std::endl;

}


void greet(std::string name) {

 std::cout << "Welcome to GitforGits, " << name << "!" << std::endl;

}


void greet(std::string name, std::string timeOfDay) {

 std::cout << "Good " << timeOfDay << ", " << name << "! Welcome to GitforGits!"
<< std::endl;

}
```

```
int main() {
 greet(); // Calls the first version
 greet("Alice"); // Calls the second version
 greet("Bob", "evening"); // Calls the third version

 return 0;
}
```

In the above given code snippet, the **greet** function is overloaded three times: with no parameters, with a name parameter, and with both name and time of day parameters. This demonstrates how function overloading can provide multiple ways to perform a similar operation (in this case, greeting) based on different inputs.

Name Mangling

Name mangling is the process by which the C++ compiler generates unique names for each function variant when it compiles your code. This is necessary because, at the binary level, each function, including its overloaded versions, must have a unique identifier. While name mangling is handled automatically by the compiler and is generally not something you need to worry about in day-to-day programming, it's important to be aware of it, especially when dealing with linking issues or interfacing with other languages.

Overloading simplifies code by allowing the same basic operation to be applied in different situations. From a programmer's perspective, it ensures that these functions are uniquely identifiable during compilation and linking. The compiler's name mangling helps with this. You can make your application more user-friendly and flexible by taking use of function overloading as you work on it.

Recipe 8: Utilizing the auto Keyword within Functions

Situation

In the previous chapter, we've seen the **auto** keyword simplifies code by allowing the compiler to deduce the type of a variable. Let us focus on how **auto** can be specifically applied within the context of functions to streamline definitions and return types, enhancing code readability and maintainability, especially in complex scenarios or when working with templates.

Practical Solution

Utilizing **auto** within functions can manifest in two primary ways: deducing the return type of functions and simplifying the declaration of lambda expressions. This becomes particularly advantageous in template programming or when dealing with types that are verbose to write out or are subject to change.

Auto in Function Return Types

C++14 introduced the ability for **auto** to be used in specifying the return type of functions, allowing the return type to be deduced from the return statements within the function. This is especially useful in template functions or when the return type is complex and cumbersome to specify explicitly.

Following is the example of **auto** for deducing return types:

```
template<typename T, typename U>

auto add(T t, U u) -> decltype(t + u) { // The trailing return type specifies the type

 return t + u; // The actual return type is deduced from the operation

}


int main() {

 auto result = add(1, 2.5); // Uses auto for both the function return type and the variable type

 std::cout << "The result is: " << result << std::endl; // result is deduced to be a double

 return 0;

}
```

Auto in Lambda Expressions

Lambda expressions benefit significantly from **auto**, as they often involve types that are determined by the context in which they are used. By employing **auto** in the parameter list of a lambda, you can write more generic and reusable lambda expressions.

Following is the example of **auto** in lambda expressions:

```
std::vector<int> values = {1, 2, 3, 4, 5};

std::for_each(values.begin(), values.end(), [](auto value) {

 std::cout << value << " ";

});

std::cout << std::endl;
```

In the above given code snippet, the lambda expression uses **auto** for its parameter, making it adaptable to work with any type of value in the container. The utilization of **auto** within functions and lambda expressions significantly streamlines C++ code, reducing verbosity and the potential for errors due to type mismatches.

Summary

We have covered all the basics of function usage in C++20 in this chapter with an emphasis on improving code readability, efficiency, and flexibility. Beginning with a knowledge of inline and constexpr functions, we've seen how to optimize function calls and enable compile-time evaluations, allowing for more efficient code execution. The addition of lambda expressions enhanced our toolkit by allowing for concise, on-the-spot function declarations, which are especially valuable in the context of algorithms or event-driven programming. The exploration of function pointers and functors expanded our capacity to pass behavior as parameters, resulting in a dynamic approach to callbacks and higher-order functions.

Continuing our chapter, we looked at the potential of templates within functions, demonstrating how to achieve type agnosticism while maximizing code reusability across many data contexts. The learnings of standard library functions and algorithms revealed the wide pre-built solutions available for common programming jobs, underlining the need of using these tools to produce efficient, clean, and tested code. Custom error handling in functions presented ways for robust and dependable software development, ensuring that our programs can gracefully handle unexpected events. The concept of function overloading, along with an understanding of name mangling, exposed C++'s polymorphism capabilities, allowing us to define several behaviors using a single function name and varied parameter types. Finally, the use of the auto keyword within functions demonstrated the shift toward type inference, which simplified code syntax while improving maintainability and readability.

An important goal of this chapter has been to introduce you to advanced function approaches in C++20 in order to increase code efficiency, readability, and reusability. The skills we've learned in this chapter will allow us to build C++ applications that are more expressive, dynamic, and type-safe; this will give us the confidence to take on the most difficult programming problems.

CHAPTER 3: OBJECT-ORIENTED PROGRAMMING IN ACTION

Introduction

The goal of this chapter is to immerse you in the fundamentals of Object-Oriented Programming (OOP) using C++20, with an emphasis on practical applications and the intricacies of OOP concepts. This chapter provides a detailed troubleshooting to grasping the fundamental parts of OOP, such as classes and objects, constructors and destructors, and the complexities of copy and move semantics, as described in the Rule of Three and the Rule of Five. Through a series of recipes, you will learn how to use classes and objects to encapsulate data and behaviors, the importance of constructors and destructors in resource management, and how to navigate the complexities of copy and move operations to ensure efficient object management.

Furthermore, we will look at advanced OOP capabilities like polymorphism and dynamic binding to show how to create flexible and scalable systems. The chapter will also go over encapsulation and access modifiers for protecting the internal state of objects, highlighting the significance of limited access in preserving object integrity. You'll look at how static members and methods share data and behaviors between instances, as well as the concept of buddy functions and classes, which break encapsulation for special access rights. Finally, the construction and implementation of abstract classes and interfaces will be covered, emphasizing their importance in building subclass contracts and fostering a plug-and-play architectural style.

By the end of this chapter, you'll learn how to use OOP principles in C++ to create strong, maintainable, and efficient applications. Through realistic examples and solutions, you'll be prepared to face real-world programming difficulties with the power of object-oriented design and C++20 capabilities.

Recipe 1: Utilize Basics of Classes and Objects

Situation

Classes and objects are the building blocks of Object-Oriented Programming (OOP), which enables you to partition data and behavior into smaller, more manageable pieces. In order to build a well-organized, scalable, and efficient application for our application, it is crucial to know how to create and utilize classes and objects. Bypassing procedural programming and stepping into the shoes of real-world entities and their interactions inside software requires this critical step.

Practical Solution

As a first step in learning object-oriented programming in C++20, let us create a simple class for the application. To begin representing a user in the GitforGits system, we may create a User class that stores all the details about the user and their actions.

```
#include <iostream>
```

```
#include <string>

class User {
private:
 std::string name;
 int id;

public:
 // Constructor
 User(std::string userName, int userId) : name(userName), id(userId) {}

 // Method to display user information
 void displayUserInfo() const {
 std::cout << "User Name: " << name << ", User ID: " << id << std::endl;
 }
};

int main() {
 // Creating an object of the User class
 User user1("Alice", 1);
```

```
// Calling a method of the object
user1.displayUserInfo();


return 0;
}
```

In the above given code snippet, the **User** class encapsulates two private data members: **name** and **id**, representing the user's name and identification number, respectively. It includes a constructor that initializes these members and a public method **displayUserInfo** to print the user's information. This basic structure demonstrates how classes and objects work together: the class serves as a blueprint, while objects are instances of this blueprint with actual data.

This approach not only makes the code more manageable and easier to understand but also lays the groundwork for leveraging more advanced OOP features like inheritance, polymorphism, and encapsulation.

Recipe 2: Apply Constructors and Destructors

Situation

The lifecycle of an object is largely controlled by constructors and destructors in the world of Object-Oriented Programming. To initialize the state of an object, the creation process calls its constructor, which is a specific member function. In contrast, destructors are notified when an object is destroyed and are responsible for cleanup tasks such as releasing resources. Properly initializing user data and efficiently managing resources are crucial for ensuring application stability and performance in our application. This is achieved by carefully implementing constructors and destructors.

Practical Solution

Constructors in C++ can be categorized into several types, including default, parameterized, and copy constructors. They enable flexibility in object initialization. We shall enhance the **User** class by adding various constructors to meet different initialization needs.

Default Constructor

These automatically initializes objects. It's crucial when you need to create an object without immediately providing detailed information.

```
User() : name("Unknown"), id(0) {} // Default constructor with initializer list
```

Parameterized Constructor

It allows passing arguments to set up your object with specific values upon creation. This constructor was introduced in our previous example.

Copy Constructor

It initializes an object using another object of the same class. It's especially important for managing deep copies of dynamically allocated resources.

```
User(const User& other) : name(other.name), id(other.id) {} // Copy constructor
```

Incorporating these constructors into the **User** class enhances its flexibility and robustness, ensuring objects are always in a valid state when they're created.

Implementing a Destructor

A destructor is defined to clean up when an object's lifetime ends. While simple projects might not always need explicit destructor logic, any class that allocates resources like memory, file handles, or network connections should properly release them to avoid leaks.

```
~User() {

 // Cleanup code here. For this example, there's nothing to clean up.

}
```

For the **User** class in the application, a destructor might seem unnecessary now, but as the application grows to handle more complex user data or external resources, having a placeholder makes it easier to manage future needs.

Special Member Function Rules

C++ has rules that automatically define certain member functions, including constructors and destructors, if you don't explicitly declare them. This is part of the language's support for "rule of zero/three/five", guiding the implementation of special member functions based on resource management needs.

Understanding when and how constructors and destructors are invoked is key to mastering C++'s OOP capabilities. Constructors not only initialize objects but can also be overloaded to provide multiple pathways for initialization, enhancing the class's usability. Destructors ensure that once an object's usefulness concludes, any system resources it consumes are properly released, preventing resource leaks that can lead to instability and bugs.

Recipe 3: Perform Copy Semantics and the Rule of Three

Situation

In C++ programming, managing how objects are copied is crucial for ensuring data integrity and resource management. This becomes especially important in complex applications like "GitforGits," where user data and other resources might be dynamically allocated. The Rule of Three is a class design principle that addresses how objects should manage resources to avoid leaks, dangling references, and other issues associated with copy operations.

Practical Solution

Understanding Copy Semantics

Copy semantics involve defining how an object can be copied, assigned, or destroyed. This includes implementing a copy constructor, copy assignment operator, and a destructor to manage deep copies of resources correctly.

- Copy Constructor - Ensures that when a new object is created as a copy of an existing object, any dynamic resources are properly duplicated.
- Copy Assignment Operator - Ensures that when an object is assigned the value of another object, any existing resources are correctly disposed of and new resources are duplicated from the source object.
- Destructor - Cleans up dynamic resources when an object goes out of scope or is deleted.

The Rule of Three

The Rule of Three states that if a class defines one of these three operations (copy constructor, copy assignment operator, or destructor), it should probably explicitly define all three. This rule is rooted in the management of resources like memory, file handles, or network connections, where incorrect handling can lead to resource leaks, dangling pointers, or other issues.

We shall apply the Rule of Three to our **User** class in our application:

```
class User {

private:
```

```
std::string name;
int* id; // Assume ID is now dynamically allocated for demonstration

public:
// Constructor
User(std::string userName, int userId) : name(userName), id(new int(userId)) {}

// Copy Constructor
User(const User& other) : name(other.name), id(new int(*other.id)) {}

// Copy Assignment Operator
User& operator=(const User& other) {
if (this != &other) { // Prevent self-assignment
name = other.name;
delete id; // Free existing resource
id = new int(*other.id); // Allocate and copy the resource
}
return *this;
}

// Destructor
```

```
~User() {
delete id; // Clean up the dynamic resource
}

// Additional functions...
};
```

In this enhanced **User** class, the dynamic allocation of the **id** necessitates a deep copy for both the copy constructor and copy assignment operator to ensure each **User** object manages its copy of the resource. The destructor then cleans up the resource when a **User** object is destroyed.

Rule of Three and Modern C++

While the Rule of Three remains foundational, modern C++ has introduced smart pointers (e.g., **std::unique_ptr**) that automate resource management, potentially reducing the need to manually implement all three operations. However, understanding the Rule of Three is crucial for scenarios where manual resource management is necessary or when working with legacy code that does not use smart pointers. It ensures that your application handles copying and assignment of objects in a way that prevents resource leaks, dangling pointers, and other common issues associated with dynamic resource management.

Recipe 4: Perform Move Semantics and the Rule of Five

Situation

Particularly in high-performance applications like "GitforGits," efficient resource management and ensuring rapid, reliable object transfers are of the utmost importance in modern C++ programming. Here, the Rule of Five and the semantics of moves become relevant. Performance can be significantly enhanced by using move semantics to transfer resources from one temporary object to another, instead of copying them. An object's behavior during copying, relocation, and destruction can be controlled by following the Rule of Five, a principle that ensures resource safety and efficiency through the implementation of five special member functions.

Practical Solution

Understanding Move Semantics

Move semantics are implemented via move constructors and move assignment operators, which "move" resources (like dynamic memory) from one object to another, leaving the source in a valid but unspecified state. This is more efficient than copying, as it avoids duplicating resources.

The Rule of Five

The Rule of Five states that if you declare or define one of the following special member functions, you should probably explicitly declare or define all five:

- Destructor
- Copy constructor
- Copy assignment operator
- Move constructor
- Move assignment operator

This rule ensures that your class correctly implements copy control, handles resources safely, and adheres to C++'s resource management idioms.

Applying Move Semantics and Rule of Five

We shall apply these concepts to our **User** class, enhancing its efficiency and safety concerning resource management.

```
#include <iostream>

#include <string>

#include <utility> // For std::move



class User {

private:

 std::string name;

 int* id; // Assume id is now dynamically allocated for demonstration
```

```
public:
 // Constructor
 User(std::string userName, int userId) : name(std::move(userName)), id(new int(userId))
{}

 // Destructor
 ~User() { delete id; }

 // Copy constructor
 User(const User& other) : name(other.name), id(new int(*other.id)) {}

 // Copy assignment operator
 User& operator=(const User& other) {
 if (this != &other) {
 name = other.name;
 delete id; // Free existing resource
 id = new int(*other.id); // Allocate and copy
 }
 return *this;
 }

 // Move constructor
```

```
User(User&& other) noexcept : name(std::move(other.name)), id(other.id) {
other.id = nullptr; // Leave source in a valid state
}

// Move assignment operator
User& operator=(User&& other) noexcept {
if (this != &other) {
name = std::move(other.name);
delete id; // Free existing resource
id = other.id; // Transfer ownership
other.id = nullptr; // Leave source in a valid state
}
return *this;
}

void displayUserInfo() const {
std::cout << "User Name: " << name << ", User ID: " << *id << std::endl;
}
};
```

In this enhanced **User** class, dynamic memory allocation for the **id** demonstrates the need for careful resource management. The implementation of the Rule of Five ensures that **User** objects can be safely copied, moved, and destroyed without leaking resources or encountering undefined behavior.

Recipe 5: Implement Polymorphism and Dynamic Binding

Situation

One of the fundamental ideas of object-oriented programming is polymorphism, which allows for several data types to be represented by a single interface. Virtual functions, which enable dynamic binding, are usually used to accomplish polymorphism in C++. At runtime, the type of the object itself determines which function is invoked, rather than the type of the reference or pointer that references it. Incorporating polymorphism into our application will significantly improve the code's scalability and flexibility, particularly when handling a hierarchy of user types or actions that may necessitate different implementations depending on the runtime object.

Practical Solution

Understanding Polymorphism

Polymorphism allows for treating objects of different classes through the same interface, provided they are derived from the same base class. This is particularly useful in our application for creating a unified interface for different user actions or roles within the system.

Dynamic Binding with Virtual Functions

Dynamic binding is achieved in C++ using virtual functions. Declaring a function as virtual in a base class signals that the function is intended to be overridden in derived classes, and the version of the function that gets called is determined at runtime based on the actual type of the object.

Implementing User Hierarchy

Consider a simplified scenario in our application where we have a base class **User** and two derived classes: **Administrator** and **RegularUser**. Each type of user will greet differently upon login.

```
#include <iostream>

#include <memory>

#include <vector>
```

```
class User {
public:
 virtual void greet() const {
 std::cout << "Welcome to GitforGits, generic user!" << std::endl;
 }
 virtual ~User() = default; // Ensure proper cleanup with a virtual destructor
};

class Administrator : public User {
public:
 void greet() const override {
 std::cout << "Welcome to GitforGits, administrator!" << std::endl;
 }
};

class RegularUser : public User {
public:
 void greet() const override {
 std::cout << "Welcome to GitforGits, regular user!" << std::endl;
 }
```

```
};

void greetUser(const User& user) {
 user.greet();
}

int main() {
 Administrator admin;
 RegularUser regular;

 greetUser(admin); // Outputs: Welcome to GitforGits, administrator!
 greetUser(regular); // Outputs: Welcome to GitforGits, regular user!

 return 0;
}
```

In the above given code snippet, both **Administrator** and **RegularUser** override the **greet** function of the **User** base class. The **greetUser** function, which takes a reference to a **User**, can call **greet** on any **User** object, and thanks to dynamic binding, the correct version of **greet** is called based on the actual type of the object passed. This demonstrates polymorphism in action, where a single interface (**greet**) is used to interact with objects of different types.

Recipe 6: Use Encapsulation and Access Modifiers

Situation

In our exploration of object-oriented programming in C++, encapsulation stands out as a paradigm that combines data (attributes) and methods (functions) that operate on the data into a single unit known as a class, while restricting access to certain of the object's components. Not only is it about encapsulating data and the functions that process it, but it's also about protecting an object's internal state from outside interference. Encapsulation in C++ is accomplished using the available access modifiers: private, protected, and public. To promote data integrity and minimize the danger of unexpected behavior, they allow us specify the scope and visibility of class members, which ensures that sensitive data remains concealed from outside access.

Practical Solution

Implementing Encapsulation

We shall refine our **User** class from the application to demonstrate encapsulation and the use of access modifiers effectively.

```
class User {
private:
 std::string name; // Accessible only within the class
 int id; // Accessible only within the class

public:
 User(std::string userName, int userId) : name(userName), id(userId) {}

 // Public method to access private data
 void displayUserInfo() const {
 std::cout << "User Name: " << name << ", User ID: " << id << std::endl;
}
```

```
// Setter and Getter for name - Demonstrating controlled access

void setName(std::string userName) {

if (!userName.empty()) {

name = userName;

}

// Additional validation or modification logic can go here

}


std::string getName() const {

return name;

}


// Note: Similar setter and getter methods can be implemented for 'id'

};
```

In this improved version of the **User** class, both the **name** and **id** attributes are marked as **private**, meaning they cannot be accessed directly from outside the class. This encapsulation ensures that the **User** objects' states can only be modified through a controlled interface—here, represented by the **setName** and **getName** methods, and any other methods you choose to expose publicly. This approach not only safeguards the data from unintended access and modification but also allows for validation and processing within the setter methods, ensuring that the object always remains in a valid state.

Understanding Access Modifiers

- Private: Members declared as private are accessible only within the class itself. Use this for data and methods that should not be exposed to the outside.

- Protected: Members declared as protected are accessible within the class, by derived classes, and by friend classes. This is less restrictive than private but more so than public, offering a balance between accessibility and protection.
- Public: Members declared as public are accessible from any part of the program. Use this for methods and properties that need to be accessed freely, like interfaces to your class.

You may ensure that your objects remain in a consistent state and reduce the likelihood of defects by selectively making some elements of your class public, protected, or private. Our growing application exemplifies how secure, robust, and maintainable object-oriented software development is built upon encapsulation and the prudent use of access modifiers.

Recipe 7: Declare and Call Static Members and Methods

Situation

For example, suppose we'd like to know how many User objects the "GitforGits" app has generated. This tally does not pertain to any particular user, but rather to the class User as a whole. To accomplish this, we can make use of static members, which allow us to create a variable at the class level that is shared by all instances. Furthermore, it would be helpful to have a class-level method that can be used to retrieve the total number of users, for example, instead of having to create a User object. To do this, we can use static methods to work with static data or execute operations that are important to classes.

Practical Solution

Static members and methods in a class are shared among all instances of that class, acting at the class level rather than the instance level. This feature of object-oriented programming in C++ is particularly useful for scenarios where you want to maintain a piece of data consistently across all objects of a class or invoke functionality without necessarily having an instance of the class. In the context of our application, static members could be used to track global states or properties related to the application, such as the number of active users or version information.

Implementing Static Members

First, we must add a static member to our **User** class to count the number of users. We will also introduce a static method to access this count.

```
#include <iostream>

#include <string>
```

```
class User {
private:
 std::string name;
 static int userCount; // Static member to keep track of the number of User objects
created

public:
 User(std::string userName) : name(userName) {
 userCount++; // Increment user count whenever a new User object is created
 }

 ~User() {
 userCount--; // Decrement user count when a User object is destroyed
 }

 static int getUserCount() { // Static method to access the user count
 return userCount;
 }

 void displayUserInfo() const {
 std::cout << "User Name: " << name << std::endl;
```

```
}
};

int User::userCount = 0; // Define and initialize static member outside the class

int main() {
 User alice("Alice");
 User bob("Bob");

 std::cout << "Total Users: " << User::getUserCount() << std::endl; // Calling static
method

 return 0;
}
```

In the above given code snippet, **userCount** is a static member variable of the **User** class, initialized to 0. Every time a **User** object is created, the constructor increments **userCount**, and every time a **User** object is destroyed, the destructor decrements it. The static method **getUserCount** provides access to this count without needing an instance of **User**.

Understanding Static Members

- Static Member Variables: Shared across all instances of the class. They are useful for representing data that is common to all objects of that class.
- Static Methods: Can be called without an instance of the class. They can only access static members or other static methods.

Static members and methods are accessed using the class name and the scope resolution operator ::, as shown with **User::getUserCount()**. This emphasizes that these members belong to the class itself rather than to any instance of the class. This capability is invaluable in situations where you need to maintain global state or provide utilities related to a class in your "GitforGits" application.

Recipe 8: Create Friend Functions and Friend Classes

Situation

There may be times when the application needs to grant access to secret and protected members of another class to an external function or class. In situations like this, knowing how friend functions and classes work is crucial. Using these C++ capabilities, trusted non-member functions or classes can break the encapsulation restrictions in a controlled manner and access a class's secret and protected areas. With careful use of these features, you can perform activities that need access to a class's internals without making them public.

Practical Solution

Understanding Static Members

Static members of a class in C++ are shared across all instances of the class. They belong to the class itself rather than any object instance and can be accessed without creating an instance of the class. Static members are useful for storing class-wide information, and static methods can access only static members.

Implementing Friend Functions and Friend Classes

We shall consider an enhanced version of the **User** class where we want to implement a functionality that allows an external function and class to access its private data. This could be useful for operations like serialization, where an external utility needs to access an object's state without altering the class's public interface.

```
#include <iostream>

#include <string>


class User;


class UserLogger {
```

```
public:
 static void logUserInfo(const User& user);
};

class User {
private:
 std::string name;
 int id;

 // Declaring a friend function
 friend void displayUserInfo(const User& user);

 // Declaring a friend class
 friend class UserLogger;

public:
 User(std::string userName, int userId) : name(userName), id(userId) {}
};

// Friend function definition
void displayUserInfo(const User& user) {
```

```
 std::cout << "User Name: " << user.name << ", User ID: " << user.id << std::endl;
}

// Friend class method definition
void UserLogger::logUserInfo(const User& user) {
 std::cout << "[LOG] User Name: " << user.name << ", User ID: " << user.id <<
std::endl;
}

int main() {
 User alice("Alice", 1);
 displayUserInfo(alice); // Direct access to private members of User
 UserLogger::logUserInfo(alice); // Access through a friend class

 return 0;
}
```

In the above given sample program, **displayUserInfo** is a non-member function that has been granted access to the **User** class's private members via the **friend** keyword, allowing it to read **User**'s private data and display user information. Similarly, **UserLogger** is a friend class that has a static method **logUserInfo**, which also accesses the private data of **User**. This setup demonstrates how friend functions and classes can interact closely with a class while maintaining the encapsulation of its members from the rest of the program.

Key Takeaway

- Friend functions and classes are powerful tools for specific scenarios where direct access to a class's private or protected members is justified.

- Use these features sparingly and thoughtfully, as they can compromise encapsulation and make code maintenance more challenging by creating tight coupling between classes or functions.

Recipe 9: Create Abstract Classes and Interfaces

Creating abstract classes and interfaces is a fundamental aspect of designing flexible and extendable object-oriented software. In the context of our "GitforGits" application, abstract classes and interfaces allow us to define a contract for a group of related classes, ensuring they provide implementations for certain behaviors or functionalities. This approach is pivotal in creating a modular architecture where components can be developed, tested, and maintained more independently.

Situation

The necessity for a well-structured framework becomes more obvious as our application expands to include more functions. A technique to establish and enforce specific functionality across various portions of the application is using abstract classes and interfaces. Although C++ lacks interfaces compared to languages like Java, we can accomplish the same goals by utilizing abstract classes. These classes consist of pure virtual functions for all member functions. Using this method, we were able to define a consistent and transparent interface for all of our system's parts.

Practical Solution

Defining Abstract Class

An abstract class in C++ is created by declaring at least one function as a pure virtual function, which is denoted by **= 0** at the end of its declaration. Such a class cannot be instantiated directly but can be used as a base class for other classes that implement the pure virtual functions.

```
class GitOperation {

public:

 virtual void execute() const = 0; // Pure virtual function makes GitOperation abstract

 virtual ~GitOperation() {} // Virtual destructor for safe polymorphic deletion

};
```

Implementing Derived Classes

To use our abstract class, we derive concrete classes from it and implement the pure virtual functions. This allows different types of git operations to be executed polymorphically.

```
class PushOperation : public GitOperation {

public:

 void execute() const override {

 std::cout << "Performing a 'push' operation." << std::endl;

 }

};


class PullOperation : public GitOperation {

public:

 void execute() const override {

 std::cout << "Performing a 'pull' operation." << std::endl;

 }

};
```

Using Interfaces to Define a Contract

We might use an abstract class to define a common interface for all git operations, ensuring that each operation knows how to execute itself. This approach not only provides clarity and consistency across the codebase but also allows for flexibility in adding new types of operations without altering existing code.

```
void performOperation(const GitOperation& operation) {

 operation.execute(); // Polymorphic call to execute

}
```

```
int main() {
 PushOperation push;
 PullOperation pull;

 performOperation(push); // Outputs: Performing a 'push' operation.
 performOperation(pull); // Outputs: Performing a 'pull' operation.

 return 0;
}
```

In this setup, **performOperation** can accept any object of a class derived from **GitOperation** and call its **execute** method, demonstrating polymorphism in action. This design allows for new git operations to be added with minimal changes to the existing code, showcasing the power of abstract classes (interfaces) in creating flexible and maintainable software architectures.

Key Takeaway

- Abstract classes serve as a blueprint for other classes, defining a set of functionalities that derived classes must implement.
- By leveraging abstract classes, our application can ensure consistency across different components or modules, making the system easier to understand, extend, and maintain.
- This approach promotes a design where the specific details of how an operation is performed are encapsulated within each derived class, adhering to the principles of encapsulation and modularity.

Summary

This chapter in overall applied object-oriented programming techniques to our sample application. To properly simulate real-world entities, we started by laying the groundwork with classes and objects that encapsulated data and behaviors. The chapter through constructors and destructors increased our grasp of object lifecycle management, emphasizing the need of properly initializing and cleaning up resources to avoid leaks and ensure system stability.

The research progressed to more advanced subjects such as copy and move semantics, which demonstrated the Rule of Three and the Rule of Five for smoothly managing object copying and resource ownership. We explored polymorphism and dynamic binding, demonstrating the capability of virtual functions to provide flexible and scalable code architectures. Encapsulation and access modifiers stressed the necessity of preserving internal state and regulating access to class members, resulting in more robust and maintainable code. The explanation of static members and methods shed light on their utility in data sharing between instances, whilst buddy functions and classes provided a more sophisticated approach to accessing private and protected members as needed. Finally, the development of abstract classes and interfaces showed the need of providing contracts for subclasses in promoting a plug-and-play design that improves modularity and extensibility.

This complete exploration of OOP principles in C++ not only improved our ability to create well-structured and fast object-oriented applications, but it also laid a solid foundation for developing complex software systems. Chapter 3 has provided us with the knowledge and abilities necessary to effectively use OOP concepts, guaranteeing that the application and any future projects are built on strong, object-oriented principles.

CHAPTER 4: EFFECTIVE USE OF STANDARD TEMPLATE LIBRARY (STL)

Introduction

The Standard Template Library is one of C++'s most potent features, and this chapter will teach you how to use it effectively. Efficient C++ programming relies on the STL's extensive components, which are covered in this chapter. These components include containers, iterators, algorithms, and smart pointers. Each recipe is intended to address specific scenarios and provide practical answers, allowing you to solve complicated issues with elegance and efficiency.

We will start by looking at the core ideas of containers and iterators, which are required for handling collections of objects in memory. Understanding these ideas is critical because they are utilized extensively throughout the STL for data storage and processing. Following that, we will look at dynamic arrays given by the STL, such as vectors, and illustrate how they're more flexible and useful than regular arrays. The subject will expand to lists and forward_lists, emphasizing their benefits in circumstances involving frequent insertions and deletions.

Associative containers, such as maps and sets, will be explored for their unique ability to store and retrieve data via key-value associations while optimizing for search operations. We will also look at the actual applications of stack and queue for managing data in precise order required. The chapter also delves into STL's sorting, searching, and updating algorithms, demonstrating how they simplify complex operations on data collections.

Predicates and lambdas, which allow for more personalized and concise code expressions, will be used extensively to customize algorithms. Smart pointers will be examined in terms of their significance in modern memory management, including how they avoid memory leaks and dangling pointers. Finally, we will learn how to handle exceptions in the STL to ensure that applications are robust and error-resistant.

After finishing this chapter, you will have a good understanding of the STL's flexible features and be prepared to use them to make C++ programs that are easier to maintain, run faster, and scale.

Recipe 1: Explore Containers and Iterators

Situation

Data collection and management efficiency is critical in any powerful C++ program, including our current application. Object and data structure collections can be safely stored with the help of the Standard Template Library's (STL) container classes. The combination of these containers with iterators, which provide access to elements within, makes for sophisticated data management and manipulation capabilities. To make the most of the STL's capabilities for dynamic data organization and access, it is essential to know how to use containers and iterators efficiently.

Practical Solution

Understanding Containers

The STL provides several types of containers, each optimized for different use cases:

- Sequence Containers (e.g., **vector**, **list**, **deque**) manage collections of objects in a sequential manner.
- Associative Containers (e.g., **set**, **map**) automatically sort elements and provide fast lookup of elements.
- Unordered Containers (e.g., **unordered_set**, **unordered_map**) store elements without any specific order but allow for efficient hash-based lookups.

For our application, using a **vector** could be ideal for storing a dynamic list of user actions or comments, given its random-access capability and efficient dynamic resizing.

Exploring Iterators

Iterators are used to point to elements within containers, providing a way to iterate over a container without exposing its internal structure. There are several types of iterators, including:

- Input/Output Iterators: For reading and writing sequential data.
- Forward Iterators: For single-pass access in one direction.
- Bidirectional Iterators: Like forward iterators but can move backward as well.
- Random Access Iterators: Support full, bidirectional navigation and can jump any number of steps at a time.

Following is the sample program with vector and Iterators:

```
#include <iostream>

#include <vector>


int main() {

 std::vector<std::string> gitforGitsActions{"commit", "push", "pull", "branch"};


 // Using an iterator to access and print elements
```

```
for (std::vector<std::string>::iterator it = gitforGitsActions.begin(); it !=
gitforGitsActions.end(); ++it) {

std::cout << *it << std::endl;

}


// C++11 and onwards allows for a simpler syntax using range-based for loops and
auto keyword

for (const auto& action : gitforGitsActions) {

std::cout << action << std::endl;

}


return 0;

}
```

In the above given code snippet, we manage a dynamic array of strings, each representing a user action in the application, using a **vector**. Iterators are then used to traverse this container, demonstrating both traditional and range-based for loop syntaxes enabled by C++11, showcasing their ease of use and readability.

Recipe 2: Implementing Dynamic Arrays in STL

Situation

Modern C++ programs rely on dynamic arrays, which allow for efficient management of collections of elements and can be resized as needed. As an implementation of dynamic arrays, the vector class in the Standard Template Library (STL) offers a sophisticated and user-friendly interface for managing collections whose sizes might change over time. To improve the administration of user data, comments, or any list of pieces that needs to be added or removed often, while keeping memory allocation and index access continuous, vector can be used in our application.

Practical Solution

Understanding vector

A **vector** in C++ STL is a sequence container that encapsulates dynamic size arrays. It supports random access to elements, which means elements can be accessed directly using indices. **vector** automatically manages its storage, resizing itself as needed, making it a highly flexible alternative to static arrays.

Key Features and Operations with vector

- Initialization: Vectors can be initialized empty or with a predefined size and value for each element.
- Adding Elements: Elements can be added to the end of a **vector** using the **push_back** method, which automatically resizes the **vector** if necessary.
- Accessing Elements: Elements can be accessed using the **at()** method or the square brackets operator **[]**. The **at()** method includes bounds checking and throws an exception if the index is out of range.
- Iteration: Iterators or range-based for loops can be used to iterate over elements in a **vector**.
- Resizing and Capacity Management: Methods like **resize()**, **reserve()**, and **shrink_to_fit()** provide control over the size and capacity of the **vector**.

Following is the sample program to implement dynamic arrays using vectors:

```
#include <iostream>

#include <vector>



int main() {

 std::vector<std::string> comments;



 // Adding comments to the vector
```

```
comments.push_back("Initial commit");

comments.push_back("Implemented login feature");

comments.push_back("Fixed bugs reported by users");


// Accessing and printing comments

for (size_t i = 0; i < comments.size(); i++) {

std::cout << comments[i] << std::endl; // Direct access

}


// Using range-based for loop for iteration

for (const auto& comment : comments) {

std::cout << comment << std::endl;

}


// Resizing the vector

comments.resize(5, "New comment"); // Resize to 5 elements, filling new slots with
"New comment"


return 0;

}
```

In the above given sample program, a **vector** named **comments** is used to store strings representing user comments in the application. The **vector** demonstrates dynamic resizing as new comments are added. Elements are accessed using both direct indexing and range-based for loops, showcasing **vector**'s flexibility and ease of use.

Recipe 3: Making Use of List and Forward_list

Situation

In certain scenarios, you might find the need for efficient insertions and deletions from any position within a sequence of elements, which might not be as performance-friendly with vectors due to their contiguous memory allocation. Here, the Standard Template Library (STL) offers two more specialized containers: **list** and **forward_list**. The **list** provides a doubly-linked list allowing bidirectional traversal, while **forward_list** implements a singly-linked list for more size-efficient storage when forward-only iteration is sufficient. Understanding when and how to use these containers can optimize performance for specific operations like frequent insertions and deletions or when memory layout constraints are considered.

Practical Solution

Utilizing list

A **list** in C++ STL offers flexibility for frequent insertions and deletions, including operations at both ends and anywhere within the list. Since **list** is a doubly-linked list, each element maintains a link to both its previous and next elements, allowing bidirectional traversal.

Key Operations

- Insertion and Deletion: You can insert or delete elements at any position without needing to shift elements, as is necessary with contiguous storage containers.
- Traversal: You can traverse in both directions, which is particularly useful for algorithms that need to look ahead or behind without re-traversing the list.

Following is the sample program to utilize list:

```
#include <iostream>

#include <list>



int main() {
```

```
std::list<std::string> userActivities{"Logged in", "Viewed dashboard", "Logged out"};

// Inserting a new activity
userActivities.push_front("Opened app"); // Insert at the beginning
userActivities.push_back("Closed app"); // Insert at the end

// Iterating over the list
for (const auto& activity : userActivities) {
std::cout << activity << std::endl;
}

// Efficiently removing an activity
userActivities.remove("Viewed dashboard");

return 0;
}
```

Exploring forward_list

For scenarios where memory efficiency is paramount and only forward iteration is needed, **forward_list** offers a more lightweight alternative to **list**. It implements a singly-linked list, where each element points only to the next element.

Key Operations

- Insertion and Deletion: Similar to **list**, but as it's singly-linked, operations that would otherwise require backward traversal might be less straightforward or require additional steps.
- Forward Traversal: Only supports forward iteration, which can be more memory efficient in certain contexts.

Following is the sample program with forward_list:

```
#include <forward_list>

#include <iostream>


int main() {

 std::forward_list<std::string> notifications{"New message", "System update available"};


 // Inserting a new notification at the beginning (since it's singly-linked)

 notifications.push_front("Friend request");


 // Forward iteration over the forward_list

 for (const auto& notification : notifications) {

 std::cout << notification << std::endl;

 }


 // Removing an element requires a workaround for singly-linked lists

 notifications.remove("System update available");
```

```
return 0;

}
```

Both **list** and **forward_list** are essential tools in the STL for managing sequences where the performance of insertions and deletions is critical, and the trade-offs between bidirectional traversal and memory efficiency are considered.

Recipe 4: Using Associative Containers: Maps and Sets

Situation

The "GitforGits" platform requires efficient data organization and access based on key-value associations or item uniqueness. In this context, the STL's associative containers become useful. Particularly important for these goals are set and map. Elements are stored as key-value pairs in a map, which enables quick retrieval using the unique key. In contrast, a set sorts elements automatically upon addition and guarantees that they are all unique. With these containers, our application may access data in an orderly and efficient manner, which significantly improves its performance and functionality.

Practical Solution

Implementing map

A **map** is ideal for scenarios where you need to maintain a direct relationship between a key and a value, such as storing user settings or mapping user IDs to usernames.

```
#include <iostream>

#include <map>

#include <string>



int main() {

 // Create a map of user IDs to usernames
```

```
std::map<int, std::string> users;
users[1] = "Alice";
users[2] = "Bob";
users[3] = "Charlie";

// Accessing and printing a specific username by user ID
std::cout << "User with ID 2: " << users[2] << std::endl;

// Iterating over the map to print all user IDs and usernames
for (const auto& pair : users) {
std::cout << "User ID: " << pair.first << ", Username: " << pair.second << std::endl;
}

return 0;
}
```

The above sample program demonstrates how a **map** can be used to associate user IDs with usernames. The **map** automatically ensures that each key is unique and provides fast lookup capabilities.

Leveraging set

A **set** is useful when you need to keep a collection of unique items, such as tags or categories in our application, and you frequently check for the existence of items or iterate over them.

```
#include <iostream>
#include <set>
```

```
#include <string>

int main() {
 // Create a set of tags
 std::set<std::string> tags{"cpp", "stl", "programming", "tutorial"};

 // Attempting to add a duplicate tag
 auto result = tags.insert("cpp"); // Insert returns a pair, where the second element is a
bool indicating success
 if (!result.second) {
 std::cout << "Tag 'cpp' already exists." << std::endl;
 }

 // Iterating over the set to print all tags
 for (const auto& tag : tags) {
 std::cout << tag << " ";
 }
 std::cout << std::endl;

 return 0;
}
```

This **set** example illustrates how to manage a collection of unique tags. The **set** automatically sorts the tags and ensures no duplicates, simplifying the management of such collections. Both **map** and **set** are powerful associative containers that serve different needs in managing collections based on unique keys or ensuring uniqueness among elements.

Recipe 5: Applied Use of Stack and Queue

Situation

Some features of our application may necessitate data structures that handle items in a particular sequence while coding. The STL stack and queue containers are ideal for jobs like redoing actions or managing user requests, where the most recent action should be reverted first or where the oldest request should be processed before the most recent one. In contrast to queues, which process jobs in the order they were added, stacks follow a Last In, First Out (LIFO) order, which is perfect for undo mechanisms. Improving the "GitforGits" app's efficiency and user-friendliness can be as simple as learning how to use these containers.

Practical Solution

Implementing stack for Undo Functionality

A **stack** is a container adapter that allows elements to be inserted and removed from one end only. This makes it an excellent choice for implementing features like an undo mechanism in our application.

```
#include <iostream>

#include <stack>

#include <string>



int main() {

 std::stack<std::string> actions;

 actions.push("create post");

 actions.push("edit post");
```

```
actions.push("delete post");

// Undo the last action
if (!actions.empty()) {
std::cout << "Undoing: " << actions.top() << std::endl; // Shows the last action
actions.pop(); // Removes the last action
}

return 0;
}
```

In the above given code snippet, each action taken by a user is pushed onto the stack. To undo an action, you remove the most recent action from the stack, mimicking an undo functionality.

Using queue for Request Processing

A **queue** ensures that elements are processed in the order they were added. This can be particularly useful for handling user requests or tasks in our application, ensuring fairness and efficiency.

```
#include <iostream>
#include <queue>
#include <string>

int main() {
std::queue<std::string> userRequests;
userRequests.push("Request 1");
```

```
userRequests.push("Request 2");

userRequests.push("Request 3");


// Process the first request

if (!userRequests.empty()) {

std::cout << "Processing: " << userRequests.front() << std::endl; // Shows the first request

userRequests.pop(); // Removes the first request

}


return 0;

}
```

In the above given code snippet, requests are enqueued in a **queue**. Processing a request involves dequeuing the front element, ensuring requests are handled in the same order as they were received.

Recipe 6: Perform Sort, Search, and Modify Algorithms

Situation

In order to sort, search, and alter containers, the Standard Template Library (STL) provides a full set of algorithms. Without having to manually implement these algorithms, there is a standardized way to conduct common tasks, and these algorithms operate across all STL containers. Operations such as sorting user contributions, searching for particular articles, or editing a list of comments become much more efficient and easy when one knows how to use these algorithms, which significantly improves the performance and functionality of our application.

Practical Solution

Sorting with std::sort

Sorting is a fundamental operation, and **std::sort** is the go-to algorithm for rearranging elements in a sequence into a specified order. It works on random-access iterators, making it suitable for containers like **vector** and **deque**.

```
#include <algorithm>

#include <vector>

#include <iostream>


int main() {

 std::vector<int> scores {45, 95, 85, 29, 72};


 // Sorting in ascending order

 std::sort(scores.begin(), scores.end());


 std::cout << "Sorted Scores: ";

 for(int score : scores) {

 std::cout << score << " ";

 }

 std::cout << std::endl;


 return 0;
```

```
}
```

Searching with std::find

To locate an element within a container, **std::find** is used. It works with any container supporting forward iterators, such as **list**, **vector**, and even arrays, providing a versatile tool for search operations.

```
#include <algorithm>

#include <vector>

#include <iostream>


int main() {

 std::vector<std::string> tags {"cpp", "stl", "programming", "tutorial"};


 auto result = std::find(tags.begin(), tags.end(), "stl");


 if(result != tags.end()) {

 std::cout << "Found tag: " << *result << std::endl;

 } else {

 std::cout << "Tag not found." << std::endl;

 }


 return 0;

}
```

Modifying with std::transform

For performing operations on elements and storing the result, **std::transform** is incredibly useful. It applies a given function to a range of elements, which can be used for modifying elements in place or storing the results in a new container.

```
#include <algorithm>

#include <vector>

#include <iostream>


int main() {

 std::vector<int> nums {1, 2, 3, 4, 5};

 std::vector<int> squared;


 // Squaring each number and storing in squared

 std::transform(nums.begin(), nums.end(), std::back_inserter(squared), [](int n) { return n
* n; });


 std::cout << "Squared Numbers: ";

 for(int n : squared) {

 std::cout << n << " ";

 }

 std::cout << std::endl;


 return 0;
```

```
}
```

You are free to concentrate on the more abstract logic of your "GitforGits" application with the help of the stable type library's (STL) sorting, searching, and editing algorithms. Your code will be efficient, transparent, and easy to maintain if you use these standardized algorithms. Applying these algorithms to user data, posts, tags, or other material can simplify data administration and make your application more robust and responsive.

Recipe 7: Customize Algorithms with Predicates and Lambdas

Situation

There may be times when you need to modify the built-in functionality of conventional algorithms to meet your unique demands, especially as the "GitforGits" platform develops. For example, you could prefer to rank user comments by length rather than lexicographic order, or apply filters to postings according to certain criteria. This is where lambdas and predicates really shine. An algorithm's decision-making process relies on predicates, which are functions that return a boolean value. Lambdas are ideal for instantiating custom predicates since they provide a succinct way to create anonymous functions directly in their context. You can manipulate data in our application in more sophisticated and personalized ways by using these tools, which increase the power and flexibility of STL algorithms.

Practical Solution

Using Predicates

A predicate is any callable entity (function, functor, lambda) that returns a boolean value. You can use predicates to guide the behavior of algorithms, such as **std::sort**, **std::find_if**, or **std::remove_if**.

Following is the example of using a functor as a predicate to sort a vector of strings by length:

```
#include <algorithm>

#include <vector>

#include <iostream>
```

```
class CompareLength {
public:
 bool operator()(const std::string& first, const std::string& second) {
 return first.length() < second.length();
 }
};

int main() {
 std::vector<std::string> comments {"Very useful post!", "Thanks!", "Please clarify the second point."};

 // Sorting comments by length using the CompareLength predicate
 std::sort(comments.begin(), comments.end(), CompareLength());

 for (const auto& comment : comments) {
 std::cout << comment << std::endl;
 }

 return 0;
}
```

Leveraging Lambdas for Inline Customization

Lambdas provide a more straightforward and inline way to define predicates or any single-use, custom logic for STL algorithms.

Following is the example of using a lambda to filter and print specific user actions:

```
#include <algorithm>

#include <vector>

#include <iostream>


int main() {

 std::vector<std::string> actions {"login", "view_post", "logout", "create_post",
"delete_post"};


 std::cout << "Actions starting with 'l':" << std::endl;

 std::for_each(actions.begin(), actions.end(), [](const std::string& action) {

 if (action.starts_with("l")) {

 std::cout << action << std::endl;

 }

 });


 return 0;

}
```

Removing the requirement for auxiliary functions or classes and instead using predicates and lambdas to customize algorithms simplifies code while keeping logic local and legible, right alongside the algorithm application.

Recipe 8: Using Smart Pointers

Situation

The management of dynamic memory becomes increasingly important as the application's complexity increases. Memory leaks, dangling pointers, and ownership confusion are risks associated with using C++'s raw pointers for dynamic memory management. A strong answer is provided by smart pointers, which were introduced in C++11 and improved in C++20. They automate memory management and provide safer resource handling. A number of smart pointer types, including std::shared_ptr, std::weak_ptr, and std::unique_ptr, are available in the Standard Template Library (STL) to address various memory management requirements. For efficient and leak-proof C++ programs, knowing how to use these smart pointers is vital.

Practical Solution

std::unique_ptr for Exclusive Ownership

std::unique_ptr manages an object and ensures that there is only one owner of the underlying pointer. It's useful for resources that need clear, singular ownership, as it automatically deletes the object it points to when the **unique_ptr** goes out of scope.

Following is the example of using **std::unique_ptr** in our application:

```
#include <iostream>

#include <memory>


class Post {

public:

 Post() { std::cout << "Post created\n"; }

 ~Post() { std::cout << "Post destroyed\n"; }

 void display() const { std::cout << "Displaying post content\n"; }

};
```

```
int main() {
 std::unique_ptr<Post> postPtr = std::make_unique<Post>();
 postPtr->display();
 // No need to manually delete the post; it will be automatically deleted when out of scope
 return 0;
}
```

std::shared_ptr for Shared Ownership

std::shared_ptr allows multiple owners of the same pointer, which can be particularly useful in our application for objects that need to be accessed from several places. The object is destroyed when the last **shared_ptr** pointing to it is destroyed or reset.

Following is the example of using **std::shared_ptr**:

```
#include <iostream>
#include <memory>


class User {
public:
 User() { std::cout << "User created\n"; }
 ~User() { std::cout << "User destroyed\n"; }
 void display() const { std::cout << "Displaying user information\n"; }
};
```

```
int main() {
 std::shared_ptr<User> userPtr1 = std::make_shared<User>();
 std::shared_ptr<User> userPtr2 = userPtr1; // Both pointers share ownership of the
User
 userPtr1->display();
 // The User is destroyed when both userPtr1 and userPtr2 go out of scope
 return 0;
}
```

std::weak_ptr to Break Cycles

std::weak_ptr is used in conjunction with **std::shared_ptr** to solve the problem of reference cycles, which can lead to memory leaks. It holds a non-owning reference to an object that is managed by **shared_ptr**. These smart pointers significantly reduce the risk of memory leaks and dangling pointers, making resource management in our application more robust and error-free. Smart pointers also convey ownership semantics explicitly, making the code more readable and maintainable.

Summary

Through this chapter, you have learned all about the Standard Template Library (STL), an essential part of C++ that provides a wealth of predefined classes and methods for typical algorithms and data structures. We learned about the fundamentals of STL containers—vectors, lists, and maps—through a set of practical recipes designed for the application. These containers are crucial for efficiently storing and organizing data. Data can be managed in various ways depending on requirements like order, uniqueness, and access patterns; this was brought to light in the discussions around vector-based dynamic arrays, linked list operations using list and forward_list, and the use of associative containers like map and set.

The chapter also delved into container adapters that work with stack and queue, demonstrating how useful they are in situations calling for FIFO and LIFO operations, respectively. Also covered in the chapter were the core STL algorithms for finding, sorting, and editing collections, and how to make them more user-friendly by adding predicates and lambdas. The significance of memory management and the benefits of automatic resource handling in preventing leaks and dangling pointers were further highlighted throughout the recipes on smart pointers, specifically std::unique_ptr, std::shared_ptr, and std::weak_ptr. By using standardized, well-tested components for typical programming tasks, this STL trip not only makes the "GitforGits" application more efficient and resilient, but it also improves coding practice.

CHAPTER 5: EXPLORING ADVANCED C++ FUNCTIONALITIES

Introduction

The goal of this chapter is to explore the more advanced features of C++ that meet the demands of modern development, with an emphasis on code scalability, organization, and efficiency. In the context of the application structure, this chapter aims to deliver useful information and answers by showing how to make use of sophisticated capabilities to improve the app's performance and the developer's experience.

At the outset of the chapter, we cover the basics of ideas and constraints, a feature introduced in C++20 that makes using templates easier and safer by letting you put criteria on template arguments. Then, we will go into how modules may completely transform C++ code organization and sharing, leading to faster compilation times, better code encapsulation, and more reusability. In order to show how to write more clear and understandable non-blocking code, we will learn about coroutines, a feature that simplifies asynchronous programming.

Moving forward, we will learn directory and file management, demonstrating improved C++ interaction with the file system. This is crucial for many applications that need persistent data storage, as it involves reading, writing, and modifying directories and files. Additionally, the chapter delves into how std::variant, std::optional, and std::any can be utilized to handle dynamic types, optional values, and type-safe unions, respectively. These classes demonstrate how these features can enhance code flexibility and robustness.

One way to improve memory management is to use custom allocators, which allow you to tailor memory allocation algorithms to your specific needs. Feature test macros, a technique for writing portable code that can adapt to different compilers and environments, will be presented as a last tool.

When this chapter is over, you will know all there is to know about advanced C++ features and approaches, and they will be able to put that knowledge to use in the application and beyond to tackle complicated issues in an elegant and efficient manner.

Recipe 1: Implement Concepts and Constraints to Simplify Templates

Situation

C++ relies on templates for code reuse and generality. Nevertheless, complicated and difficult-to-understand error messages might result from the improper use of templates. Thanks to C++20's novel concepts, we have a potent tool for limiting template types to only those that match certain criteria. By providing explicit contracts for template parameters, leveraging notions can considerably streamline template usage for "GitforGits," whether dealing with user data processing or system configuration handling.

Practical Solution

Implementing Concepts

Concepts allow for the definition of semantic requirements for template arguments. A concept is a predicate evaluated at compile time, and it specifies constraints on template arguments.

Following is the example of defining and using a concept:

```
#include <iostream>
#include <vector>
#include <concepts>

// Define a simple concept for a type that supports increment
template<typename T>
concept Incrementable = requires(T a) {
 { ++a } -> std::same_as<T>;
 { a++ } -> std::same_as<T>;
};

// Use the concept to constrain the template parameter
template<Incrementable T>
void incrementAndPrint(T value) {
 std::cout << "Original: " << value << ", Incremented: " << ++value << std::endl;
}

int main() {
 incrementAndPrint(10); // Valid: int supports increment
 incrementAndPrint(2.5); // Valid: double supports increment
 // incrementAndPrint("test"); // Error: const char* does not satisfy Incrementable
 return 0;
}
```

In the above given code snippet, the Incrementable concept checks if a type supports the increment operation. The incrementAndPrint function template is constrained to only accept types that satisfy the Incrementable concept, ensuring type safety and clear intent.

Benefits of Using Concepts

- Concepts make templates easier to read and understand. By naming the requirements, code becomes self-documenting.

- When a type does not meet a concept's requirements, the compiler can provide clearer, more directed error messages.
- Concepts prevent misuse of templates by enforcing compile-time checks on the types used as template parameters.

Recipe 2: Using Modules to Organize C++ Codes

Situation

Over time, controlling and organizing the codebase becomes harder. Although C++'s traditional header files and preprocessor directives have long been the de facto standard for code organization and reuse, they are not without their own complications, such as long compile times and global namespace pollution. A more modern approach to these issues is introduced in C++20 with the introduction of modules, which seek to shorten build times, encapsulate implementation details, and make dependencies more explicit. This ultimately improves the code's structure and maintainability.

Practical Solution

Introduction to Modules

Modules offer a way to partition C++ code into logical units, not only at the textual level, like header files, but also at the semantic level, with clear interfaces and implementation sections. A module interface specifies which parts of the module are accessible to users, while the implementation part contains private details.

Creating a Module

To create a module in "GitforGits," you define a module interface file (.ixx or .cppm depending on the compiler) that declares the exported entities.

Following is the example on module interface (user.ixx):

```
export module user;

export class User {
public:
 User(const std::string& name) : name_(name) {}
 void displayName() const {
 std::cout << "User: " << name_ << std::endl;
```

```
 }
private:
 std::string name_;
};
```

Using a Module

Once a module is defined, it can be imported and used in other parts of the application, simplifying the inclusion of code and reducing compilation dependencies.

Following is the example of using the user module (main.cpp):

```
import user;

int main() {
 User alice("Alice");
 alice.displayName();
 return 0;
}
```

Benefits of Modules

- Modules can significantly reduce the time needed to compile a program by eliminating the need to reparse the same headers multiple times.
- By defining clear interfaces, modules help encapsulate implementation details, making your code more robust and easier to maintain.
- Modules provide a namespace-like mechanism that reduces the chances of global namespace pollution.

Adopting modules can result in cleaner code, faster build times, and a more pleasant working experience because they represent a substantial change to the organization and sharing of C++ code.

Recipe 3: Simplify Asynchronous Programming with Coroutines

Situation

Asynchronous operation management is becoming increasingly important as our application adds more real-time features like live notifications and concurrent user interactions. Code that uses the standard techniques of asynchronous programming in C++, such as callbacks, futures, and promises, can be complex and difficult to maintain. Code dealing with asynchronous activities is now more clear and readable because to C++20's introduction of coroutines, a new paradigm that simplifies asynchronous programming by allowing functions to be interrupted and resumed.

Practical Solution

Understanding Coroutines

Coroutines are functions that can suspend execution to await asynchronous operations and then resume where they left off, all without blocking the executing thread. This capability is particularly beneficial for I/O-bound operations, like fetching data over the network or accessing files, as it keeps the application responsive.

Implementing Coroutine

To use coroutines in C++, you need to include headers <coroutine> for the coroutine support library and <future> for handling asynchronous return values. Following is a simple example of a coroutine in our application that simulates fetching user data asynchronously:

```
#include <iostream>
#include <coroutine>
#include <future>

std::future<std::string> fetchUserData(int userId) {
 co_return "User Data for ID: " + std::to_string(userId);
}

int main() {
 auto futureUserData = fetchUserData(42);
 std::cout << "Fetching user data..." << std::endl;
 // Wait for the coroutine to complete and get the result
 std::cout << futureUserData.get() << std::endl;
 return 0;
}
```

In the above given code snippet, fetchUserData is a coroutine that simulates an asynchronous operation using co_return to provide the result. The future returned from the coroutine can be used to wait for the operation to complete and to retrieve the result.

Benefits of Using Coroutines

- Coroutines make asynchronous code look and behave more like synchronous code, improving its readability.
- By allowing functions to pause and resume, coroutines enable non-blocking operations, keeping your application responsive.
- Writing asynchronous code without coroutines often involves nested callbacks or complex state machines. Coroutines abstract away these complexities.

Coroutines in C++20 represent a significant advancement in simplifying asynchronous programming for applications that require efficient handling of I/O-bound operations or any tasks that benefit from non-blocking execution.

Recipe 4: Managing Files and Directories

Situation

In order to store user data, manage posts, and track application actions, our application relies on effective file and directory management. Using a combination of standard library functions and direct calls to the operating system for file management in older C++ projects can be a pain and makes the code less portable. With the improvements to the filesystem library released in C++17 and refined in C++20, a standardized method for working with directories and files was provided, making file operations more straightforward and reducing the likelihood of errors.

Practical Solution

Filesystem Library

The <filesystem> library in C++ offers comprehensive facilities for performing operations on file systems, such as creating directories, moving files, and querying file attributes. This library abstracts away platform-specific details, offering a uniform and safe interface for file system manipulation.

Basic Operations with <filesystem>

- Creating Directories: To organize user data or application logs.

```
#include <filesystem>
#include <iostream>

namespace fs = std::filesystem;

int main() {
```

```
fs::path dirPath = "GitforGitsData";
if(!fs::exists(dirPath)) {
fs::create_directory(dirPath);
std::cout << "Directory created: " << dirPath << std::endl;
}
return 0;
}
```

- Listing Files in a Directory: Useful for applications that need to process or display a list of files, such as a user's uploaded images or documents.

```
for(const auto& entry : fs::directory_iterator(dirPath)) {
std::cout << entry.path() << std::endl;
}
```

- Reading and Writing Files: Streamlining content management, like user posts or configuration settings.

```
fs::path filePath = dirPath / "user_post.txt";
std::ofstream fileOut(filePath);
fileOut << "This is a user post content." << std::endl;
fileOut.close();

std::ifstream fileIn(filePath);
std::string content((std::istreambuf_iterator<char>(fileIn)),
std::istreambuf_iterator<char>());
std::cout << "File content: " << content << std::endl;
```

- Renaming or Moving Files: For modifying user content or archiving.

```
fs::path newFilePath = dirPath / "archived_post.txt";
fs::rename(filePath, newFilePath);
```

- Removing Files or Directories: To clean up outdated data or upon user request.

```
if(fs::remove(newFilePath)) {
std::cout << "File removed successfully." << std::endl;
}
```

Key Takeaway

The filesystem library offers a robust and standardized method for working with C++'s file system, including operations such as creating and manipulating files, as well as running directory searches. These capabilities can make our application's code simpler, more portable, and easier to maintain by simplifying user-generated content, application data storage, and file management. The scalability and user experience of the application are improved by removing platform-specific details, which makes file operations robust and portable across different operating systems.

Recipe 5: Utilizing Variant, Optional, and Any

Situation

More and more often, we are faced with data that is either ambiguous or heterogeneous. The three new strong utilities in C++17, std::variant, std::optional, and std::any, enable you to handle missing user inputs, manage numerous data types in the same container, and implement functions that can return multiple types of outputs. Simplifying code logic and boosting program stability are two benefits of these kinds, which provide more expressive, safe, and standardized ways to work with such data.

Practical Solution

Using std::optional for Potentially Absent Values

std::optional represents a value that may or may not be present. It's especially useful for functions that might fail to produce a value or for optional function parameters.

Following is the example of std::optional in use:

```
#include <iostream>
#include <optional>

std::optional<std::string> fetchUserName(int userId) {
 if (userId == 1) {
 return "GitforGitsUser";
 } else {
 return std::nullopt; // Represents an absent value
 }
}

int main() {
 auto userName = fetchUserName(1);
 if (userName) {
 std::cout << "User name: " << *userName << std::endl;
 } else {
 std::cout << "User not found." << std::endl;
```

```
 }
 return 0;
}
```

Working with std::variant for Holding Multiple Types

std::variant holds a single value of one of several specified types. It's a type-safe union, ideal for variables that can represent different types over time.

Following is the example of std::variant in action:

```
#include <iostream>
#include <variant>

int main() {
 std::variant<int, float, std::string> data;
 data = 10;
 std::cout << std::get<int>(data) << std::endl;

 data = "GitforGits";
 std::cout << std::get<std::string>(data) << std::endl;

 // Use std::visit to handle all types
 std::visit([](auto&& arg) { std::cout << arg << std::endl; }, data);
 return 0;
}
```

Employing std::any for Storing Any Type

std::any can hold an instance of any type. It's useful when the exact type of the stored data is not known until runtime.

Following is the example of demonstrating std::any:

```
#include <iostream>
#include <any>

int main() {
 std::any value = 42;
 std::cout << std::any_cast<int>(value) << std::endl;

 value = std::string("A string in std::any");
```

```
std::cout << std::any_cast<std::string>(value) << std::endl;

// Check if the type is correct before casting
if (value.type() == typeid(std::string)) {
std::cout << "Value is a string." << std::endl;
}
return 0;
}
```

All the three viz, std::optional, std::variant, and std::any provides safe and versatile methods to handle data that is uncertain, heterogeneous, or dynamically typed, thus enhancing C++'s type system. These utilities improve the code's robustness and readability for our application by making it easier to handle functions with optional or multiple return types, store mixed data types, and handle various user inputs.

Recipe 6: Implementing Custom Allocators

Situation

Our application might face performance bottlenecks or specific memory usage patterns that the standard allocator does not address efficiently. For instance, the application could benefit from a pooling strategy for memory allocation to minimize fragmentation and improve allocation speed. Custom allocators provide a solution, offering the flexibility to define memory allocation behavior tailored to the application's needs.

Practical Solution

Understanding Allocators

In C++, allocators are objects responsible for abstracting memory allocation and deallocation. They are used implicitly by container classes like std::vector, std::list, and others to manage their elements' memory. By creating a custom allocator, you can control how these containers allocate and deallocate memory.

Creating a Custom Allocator

A basic custom allocator must conform to the allocator interface required by C++ containers. This interface includes member types like value_type, pointer, const_pointer, etc., and member functions for allocation (allocate) and deallocation (deallocate), among others.

Following is a simplified example of a custom allocator that uses std::malloc and std::free for memory management but could be modified to implement more complex strategies, such as pooling:

```
#include <cstdlib>
#include <memory>
#include <iostream>
#include <vector>

template<typename T>
class SimpleAllocator {
public:
 using value_type = T;

 SimpleAllocator() = default;

 template<typename U>
 constexpr SimpleAllocator(const SimpleAllocator<U>&) noexcept {}

 [[nodiscard]] T* allocate(std::size_t n) {
 if(n > std::size_t(-1) / sizeof(T)) throw std::bad_alloc();
 if(auto p = static_cast<T*>(std::malloc(n * sizeof(T)))) {
 return p;
 }
 throw std::bad_alloc();
 }

 void deallocate(T* p, std::size_t) noexcept {
 std::free(p);
 }
};

template<typename T, typename U>
bool operator==(const SimpleAllocator<T>&, const SimpleAllocator<U>&) { return
true; }
template<typename T, typename U>
bool operator!=(const SimpleAllocator<T>&, const SimpleAllocator<U>&) { return
false; }

int main() {
 std::vector<int, SimpleAllocator<int>> vec;
```

```
 vec.push_back(42);
 std::cout << "Using custom allocator. Vec size: " << vec.size() << ", first element: "
<< vec[0] << std::endl;
 return 0;
}
```

This custom allocator, SimpleAllocator, can be used with any standard container like std::vector. It provides a basic example of how you might start creating an allocator tailored to specific memory allocation patterns or performance needs.

Benefits

Using custom allocators can optimize memory usage, reduce allocation overhead, and improve performance for specific scenarios. However, designing and implementing a custom allocator requires a deep understanding of both the C++ memory model and the application's memory usage patterns. Allocators should be thoroughly tested to ensure they handle memory without leaks or errors.

Recipe 7: Applying Feature Test Macros

Situation

C++ is a dynamic language that is always changing as new features and capabilities are added with each new standard edition. If a complicated project like our application takes advantage of the newest capabilities, the code will be more efficient, easier to read, and faster. On the other hand, it becomes difficult to guarantee compatibility across many environments and compilers. With the introduction of feature test macros in C++20, a standardized method for checking the presence of targeted language or library features during compilation has been established. By making use of these macros, you can adjust your code to the capabilities of the compiler being used, making it both portable and forward-compatible.

Practical Solution

Understanding Feature Test Macros

Feature test macros are predefined macros that indicate whether a specific C++ feature is supported by the compiler. Each macro corresponds to a particular feature and is defined if and only if the compiler implements the feature. These macros are part of the <version> header file, allowing you to conditionally compile code based on feature availability.

Using Feature Test Macros

Suppose our application wants to use concepts (introduced in C++20) to make templates safer and easier to use. However, you need to ensure that the codebase remains compatible with compilers that do not yet support concepts. Feature test macros can be used to conditionally enable concept-based code or fall back to traditional template code.

Following is the example of applying feature test macros:

```
#include <version>

#ifdef __cpp_concepts
#include <concepts>
template<typename T>
requires std::integral<T>
T add(T a, T b) {
 return a + b;
}
#else
template<typename T>
T add(T a, T b) {
 static_assert(std::is_integral<T>::value, "T must be an integral type.");
 return a + b;
}
#endif

int main() {
 auto sum = add(5, 3); // Works with both C++20 compilers and older versions
 return 0;
}
```

In the above given sample program, __cpp_concepts is a feature test macro that checks if the compiler supports concepts. If supported, the function template add is defined using a concept to constrain T to integral types. If not, the function falls back to a traditional static assertion check.

Benefits of Feature Test Macros

- Code can be written to automatically take advantage of new features as compilers are updated, without breaking compatibility with older compilers.
- Ensures that code behaves consistently across different platforms and compilers by adapting to their supported features.
- Reduces the need for compiler-specific code paths, making the codebase easier to understand and maintain.

Summary

The purpose of this chapter was to go deeper into the C++20 programming language and showcase its more advanced capabilities, which enable you to build code that is more efficient, safe, and expressive. Simplifying templates from the ground up makes them more user-friendly and resistant to misuse; we started with concepts and limitations to demonstrate this. Projects like "GitforGits," which heavily utilize template-based design patterns, benefit significantly from this. Modules solved the problems with header files and preprocessor directives that had been plaguing code organization and compilation efficiency for a long time.

The exploration proceeded with coroutines, which provided a simpler method of asynchronous programming and significantly improved the application's scalability and responsiveness. With the help of the filesystem library, working with directories and files is now much easier; this makes it easier to do things like manage material in "GitforGits." The trio of std::variant, std::optional, and std::any were created to provide more robust data handling by providing flexible ways for handling uncertain, heterogeneous, or dynamically-typed data. One way to optimize memory management for portions that are crucial to performance is to use custom allocators. Finally, feature test macros were emphasized as a tool for safely utilizing new language features and assuring compatibility across different compiler versions. Projects like our application are progressing toward more innovation and technical brilliance because of C++20's enhanced capabilities, which allow you to solve complicated problems in a more beautiful and efficient way.

Chapter 6: Effective Error Handling and Debugging

Introduction

This chapter digs into important strategies and practices for improving the robustness, maintainability, and debugging capabilities of C++ applications. This chapter is primarily intended to provide you with sophisticated tools and procedures for guaranteeing code quality, stability, and performance in your projects. You will learn how to implement exception safety strategies through a series of painstakingly prepared recipes, which are critical for building robust code that gracefully manages runtime anomalies. Advanced debugging methodologies will be revealed, providing tactics that go beyond typical debugging to diagnose and resolve complicated situations rapidly.

The chapter then moves on to establish the fundamentals of logging and tracing, which are required for monitoring application behavior and troubleshooting in real-world scenarios. This includes in-depth discussions on how to implement custom exception classes to improve error reporting and management tailored to specific application needs. It goes on to learn testing software correctness using static and dynamic analysis techniques, which can detect potential faults and performance bottlenecks ahead of time. Furthermore, using assertions for debugging provides a proactive way to detecting issues early in the development cycle. Finally, implementing error handling policies for libraries and applications gives a framework for developing consistent and predictable error management solutions, which are critical for constructing dependable and user-friendly software components. The chapter's advanced themes aim to strengthen your ability to write error-free, debuggable, and high-quality C++ code, paving the way for confidently constructing sophisticated programs and libraries.

Recipe 1: Execute Exception Safety Technique

Situation

When an error occurs in C++, the code should keep running properly without wasting resources or corrupting data. This is called exception safety. This is quite important in "GitforGits," particularly in the sections of the program that handle file operations, communication over networks, or complicated data processing. Finding the sweet spot between performance, readability, and exception safety is no easy feat. Resource Acquisition Is Initialization (RAII), smart pointers, and transactional design patterns are a few of the techniques that C++ offers to make this possible.

Practical Solution

Levels of Exception Safety

- Basic Guarantee: At a minimum, ensure that invariants of components are preserved, and no resources are leaked. This often involves using smart pointers to manage resources automatically.
- Strong Guarantee: This level aims to make operations atomic; they either complete successfully or have no effect at all, rolling back to the initial state in the case of an exception.
- Nothrow Guarantee: The highest level of exception safety, where operations guarantee not to throw any exceptions, often by performing potentially throwing operations ahead of time or using nothrow versions of operations.

Use RAII and Smart Pointers

Automatically manage resources with objects that acquire resources in their constructors and release them in their destructors, ensuring clean-up even if exceptions occur.

```
#include <memory>

#include <vector>


void processFile(const std::string& filename) {

 std::unique_ptr<std::FILE, decltype(&std::fclose)> filePtr(std::fopen(filename.c_str(),
"r"), &std::fclose);

 if (!filePtr) throw std::runtime_error("Failed to open file.");

 // Use filePtr without worrying about closing the file descriptor

}
```

Transaction-Based Operations

Design operations to prepare changes without modifying the original state and commit only when all potentially throwing operations succeed.

```
#include <algorithm> // For std::copy

#include <vector>
```

```
class DataProcessor {
 std::vector<int> data;

public:
 void processData(const std::vector<int>& newData) {
 std::vector<int> tempData; // Temporary storage
 tempData.reserve(newData.size());
 // Potentially throwing operations here
 std::copy(newData.begin(), newData.end(), std::back_inserter(tempData));
 // Commit changes
 data.swap(tempData); // Strong guarantee: either succeeds or no state change
 }
};
```

Leverage Nothrow Operations and Checks

For functions that must not fail, use operations guaranteed not to throw and check preconditions beforehand.

```
void noThrowFunction() noexcept {
 // Implementation guaranteed not to throw exceptions
}
```

Key Takeaway

The RAII pattern, smart pointers, and transactional operation design allow our application to be resilient against runtime errors, which improves reliability and user experience. It is critical to strike a balance between these strategies, application performance, and code readability to guarantee a secure, efficient, and maintainable application.

Recipe 2: Perform Advanced Debugging

Situation

Through the integration of numerous services and the handling of complicated user interactions, our application has developed into a feature-rich platform. This level of complexity increases the likelihood that you will face elusive errors that are hard to replicate or comprehend with just traditional debugging tools. Runtime analysis, memory check tools, conditional breakpoints, and other advanced debugging approaches are crucial. To better understand the application's behavior and find more nuanced problems, you can use these techniques, which go beyond simple step-through debugging.

Practical Solution

Conditional Breakpoints

Conditional breakpoints halt the execution of the program when specific conditions are met, making them incredibly useful for catching bugs that occur under particular circumstances without stopping the program unnecessarily. In your IDE or debugger, set a breakpoint with a condition that evaluates to true when the suspected issue might occur. For example, halt execution when a variable reaches an unexpected value or when entering a specific part of the code.

Memory Check Tools

Memory-related issues, such as leaks or illegal accesses, can lead to erratic behavior and are often challenging to trace. Tools like Valgrind or AddressSanitizer can analyze memory usage and access in real-time, identifying problems early. Integrate these tools into your testing process. For instance, use Valgrind by running **valgrind --leak-check=full ./gitforgits_executable** to check for memory leaks.

Runtime Analysis and Profiling

Runtime profilers and analyzers offer insights into the application's execution, highlighting performance bottlenecks, threading issues, and inefficient algorithms. Utilize tools such as gprof or Intel VTune to analyze the application's performance. Look for hotspots or sections of code that consume unexpected amounts of CPU time or resources.

Logging and Tracing

Strategically placed logging can illuminate the application's flow and state prior to an issue occurring, especially for problems that are hard to reproduce interactively.

```
#include <iostream>

#include <fstream>


void logMessage(const std::string& message) {

 static std::ofstream logFile("gitforgits_debug.log");

 logFile << message << std::endl;

}


// Use logMessage throughout the code to track application flow and data state
```

Programmers can significantly improve their capacity to identify and resolve issues with "GitforGits" by making use of conditional breakpoints, memory check tools, runtime analysis, and rigorous logging. The application's stability and reliability are enhanced, along with developer efficiency and user happiness, when these strategies are employed prudently.

Recipe 3: Implement Custom Exception Classes

Situation

Because of the unique nature of developing "GitforGits," it is certain that mistakes and unusual circumstances will arise. The standard exception library in C++ includes many different sorts of exceptions, but there may be times when those types aren't enough to convey the exact nature of the issue or any other pertinent information. By letting you create exceptions that are specific to the needs of the application, custom exception classes improve the readability of catch blocks, and make it easier to log or send precise error information to the user, you may significantly improve error handling.

Practical Solution

Designing Custom Exception Classes

A well-designed custom exception class should inherit from **std::exception** or one of its subclasses, providing compatibility with the standard C++ exception handling mechanisms. It's important to override the **what()** method to return a message that describes the error condition clearly.

Following is the sample implementation for the given situation:

```
#include <stdexcept>

#include <string>


class GitforGitsException : public std::runtime_error {

public:

 GitforGitsException(const std::string& message)

 : std::runtime_error(message) {}


 // Optionally, add more constructors, member functions, or data members to carry additional context about the error

};


class UserNotFoundException : public GitforGitsException {

public:

 UserNotFoundException(const std::string& username)

 : GitforGitsException("User not found: " + username), username(username) {}
```

```
 const std::string& getUsername() const { return username; }

private:
 std::string username;
};

// Usage in application code
void findUser(const std::string& username) {
 // Simulate user not found
 throw UserNotFoundException(username);
}

int main() {
 try {
 findUser("Alice");
 } catch (const UserNotFoundException& e) {
 std::cerr << "Error: " << e.what() << std::endl;
 // Handle exception, e.g., log error, notify user, etc.
 }
 return 0;
```

```
}
```

In the above given sample program, **GitforGitsException** is a custom exception class derived from **std::runtime_error**, designed to be a base class for more specific GitforGits-related exceptions. **UserNotFoundException** is a more specialized exception that includes the username that could not be found, demonstrating how custom exceptions can carry additional context about the error situation. Custom exception classes provide a powerful mechanism for expressing specific error conditions in a manner that is directly relevant to the application's domain.

Recipe 4: Validate Program Correctness with Static and Dynamic Analysis

Situation

Verifying the integrity and accuracy of the code is getting more and more difficult. The codebase is susceptible to bugs, performance concerns, and possible security vulnerabilities, all of which can compromise the application's integrity and negatively impact the user experience. Static and dynamic analysis techniques can help you reduce such risks. Both tools are useful for evaluating and checking the correctness of programs, but one does it before the program is executed (static analysis) and the other does it while the program is running (dynamic analysis). The quality and robustness of code can be significantly improved by learning how to use these tools.

Practical Solution

Understanding Static Analysis

Static analysis involves examining the source code without executing it. The goal is to detect potential errors, code smells, and security vulnerabilities early in the development cycle. Static analysis tools can catch a wide range of issues, from syntax errors and typos to complex problems like memory leaks, race conditions, and unreachable code.

Static Analysis with Clang-Tidy

Clang-Tidy is a versatile static analysis tool that can help identify common mistakes or non-idiomatic practices. Following is the sample program:

```
#include <vector>
```

```
int main() {
 std::vector<int> data{1, 2, 3};
 auto it = data.begin();
 for (; it != data.end(); ++it) {
 // Potentially unsafe operation or logic error
 }
 // Example issue: Unused variable 'it' after loop
 return 0;
}
```

Integrate Clang-Tidy into your build system or IDE. For a command-line setup, you might run as below:

```
clang-tidy main.cpp -- -std=c++20
```

This command analyzes **main.cpp** for potential issues according to the enabled checks.

Understanding Dynamic Analysis

Dynamic analysis assesses the program while it's running, offering insights into its behavior under various conditions. This includes monitoring for memory leaks, checking for undefined behavior, and analyzing performance characteristics. Dynamic analysis is crucial for identifying issues that only manifest during execution, such as runtime errors and resource mismanagement.

Dynamic Analysis with Valgrind

Valgrind is a tool for memory debugging, memory leak detection, and profiling. Followin is the sample program describing a potential issue for dynamic analysis:

```
#include <cstdlib>


void potentiallyLeakyFunction() {
```

```
int* dynamicArray = new int[100]; // Memory allocated but not freed
// Logic that might forget to free dynamicArray
}

int main() {
potentiallyLeakyFunction();
return 0;
}
```

To detect memory leaks, you would compile your program (with debugging symbols enabled, using **-g**) and then run Valgrind:

```
g++ -g -o my_app main.cpp
valgrind --leak-check=full ./my_app
```

Valgrind's output will report the memory leak caused by the dynamically allocated array not being freed.

By including dynamic and static analysis tools, such as Clang-Tidy and Valgrind, into your continuous integration and continuous delivery processes, you may enhance code quality and reliability by identifying and fixing potential errors early on. Although these tools can be easily integrated without modifying your code, they offer useful insights that can be used to enhance both your current and future code.

Recipe 5: Leverage Assertions for Debugging

Situation

What if there was a sophisticated system for managing users, wherein different processes relied on the presence of a user's profile in the database? Undefined behavior or difficult-to-trace issues may result from accidentally calling a function with a non-existent user ID. To make it crystal evident during development when this assumption is ever violated, you can use assertions to enforce the existence of the user ID.

Practical Solution

Understanding Assertions

Assertions are implemented via the **assert** macro from the **<cassert>** header in C++. The **assert** statement takes a condition as its argument, which is expected to evaluate to true. If the condition evaluates to false, the program will print an error message to the standard error stream and terminate execution.

Implementing Assertions

Consider a function that retrieves user data. An assertion could ensure that the user ID passed to the function corresponds to an existing user.

```
#include <cassert>

#include <iostream>

#include <unordered_map>


std::unordered_map<int, std::string> userData = {{1, "Alice"}, {2, "Bob"}};


void fetchUserData(int userId) {

 // Assert that the userId must exist in userData

 assert(userData.find(userId) != userData.end() && "User ID does not exist.");


 // If the program continues past this point, it's safe to use userId

 std::cout << "Fetched data for user " << userData[userId] << std::endl;

}
```

```
int main() {
 fetchUserData(1); // Valid case
 fetchUserData(3); // Triggers assert and terminates the program

 return 0;
}
```

Best Practices for Using Assertions

- Use Assertions for Internal Invariants: Assertions are best used to check for conditions within the program that should logically always be true, not for validating external input or handling runtime errors.
- Disable Assertions in Production: By default, assertions are enabled. However, they can be disabled for production builds by defining **NDEBUG** before including the **<cassert>** header. This prevents the performance overhead and potential exposure of sensitive information through error messages.

With assertions, you can be sure the program is only running under valid conditions, which means fewer problems and undefined behavior. It is essential to have robust error handling and validation procedures in place to supplement assertions, particularly when dealing with user input and other external data.

Recipe 6: Design Error Handling Policies for Libraries and Applications

Situation

Each part of our application has the ability to handle a unique type of error, such as a database problem, a network outage, or incorrect user input. The only way to handle these issues consistently and thoroughly throughout the program is to have a policy in place. Not only do these policies make debugging and maintenance easier, but they also guarantee that the program will behave predictably even when faced with errors.

Practical Solution

Categorize Errors

- Recoverable Errors: Errors from which the program can recover, such as temporary network downtimes or invalid user inputs. These typically require user notification and the opportunity to retry the operation.
- Unrecoverable Errors: Critical issues that prevent the program from continuing, such as a corrupted database or a missing system dependency. These might require logging the error details and terminating the application gracefully.

Error Handling Mechanisms

- For libraries, prefer throwing exceptions to report errors. Exceptions allow calling code to handle errors in a context-specific manner. Ensure exceptions are well-documented and consistent.
- For applications, especially at the user interface level, catch exceptions and translate them into user-friendly error messages. Log detailed error information for debugging purposes.

Following is the sample program to implement a Unified Error Handling Strategy

```
// Example: Unified error handling function

void handleError(const std::exception& e) {

 // Log the error for developers

 std::cerr << "Error: " << e.what() << std::endl;


 // For user-facing components, translate to a user-friendly message

 // displayErrorMessage("An unexpected error occurred. Please try again.");

}


// Example: Using the strategy in a network operation

try {

 performNetworkOperation();
```

```
} catch (const NetworkException& e) {
 handleError(e);
 // Optionally, retry or provide feedback to the user
} catch (const std::exception& e) {
 handleError(e);
 // Handle other exceptions or terminate
}
```

By distinguishing between recoverable and unrecoverable errors, adopting appropriate handling mechanisms, and after applying all these strategies aids in maintaining the application's integrity during runtime and also facilitates easier debugging and maintenance by you.

Summary

In sum, the tools and knowledge presented in this chapter provides you with a solid foundation upon which to build more resilient and easily maintainable C++ applications. We began by investigating ways to protect applications from unanticipated mistakes, with an emphasis on implementing exception safety approaches to maintain consistent application states and proper management of resources. In order to construct robust software that can elegantly handle real-world complexity and human interactions, this foundation was vital. Conditional breakpoints, memory check tools, and runtime analysis are critical to a well-maintained codebase, and advanced debugging techniques have added new methods to our toolbox for finding and fixing complex issues that traditional debugging approaches could miss.

To further aid in the diagnosis of problems in production settings and the monitoring of application activity, the chapter delves into the establishment of logging and tracing techniques. The ability to properly convey difficulties within the application and to its users was enhanced by implementing bespoke exception classes, which allowed for more expressive and meaningful error reporting. We improved the code's quality and performance by proactively finding and fixing possible bugs through the deep dive of static and dynamic analysis. A proactive debugging strategy that helps you detect logical flaws early in the development process is leveraging assertions. In conclusion, a structured approach to error management was offered by the establishment of error handling policies for libraries and applications. This method guarantees that the program will act predictably under bad conditions and will offer users a seamless experience. In this chapter, one pillar that stood out was the need of writing code that is clear, manageable, and error-resistant.

This is essential for creating trustworthy C++ applications that can handle the demands of modern software development.

CHAPTER 7: CONCURRENCY AND MULTITHREADING

Introduction

Exploring parallel computing in C++ apps is something we need to master so that we can improve speed, responsiveness, and scalability. The intricacies of concurrent programming are broken down into manageable chunks in this chapter, which offers helpful hints and solutions for making the most of C++'s threading features. Beginning with the std::thread foundations, we will go into the ins and outs of threading to learn how to generate, manage, and synchronize threads to do tasks simultaneously, making our application far more efficient to execute.

To keep data intact and avoid race circumstances when numerous threads access shared resources, the concurrency trip continues with a thorough examination of synchronization methods, including atomics, locks, and mutexes. In concurrent programs, thread safety is of the utmost importance. This chapter provides solutions and best practices to avoid common errors in multithreaded programming. Further streamlining the process of optimizing our application for concurrent operations, we will also explore the parallel algorithms included in C++20. These algorithms permit the easy construction of parallel execution patterns.

A complete toolbox for developing strong multithreaded programs is provided, including coverage of managing the thread lifecycle and state, understanding and using futures and promises for asynchronous task execution, and implementing task-based concurrency. Particular emphasis is placed on avoiding deadlocks, which are prevalent in concurrent programming, by providing examples of strategies that do just that. This chapter teaches you how to use C++'s concurrency and multithreading features to their fullest potential through examples and explanations. This will allow them to build efficient, scalable, and high-performance apps that can handle today's software problems.

Recipe 1: Perform Basic Threading with std::thread

Situation

Making use of the host system's numerous cores becomes crucial when our application starts to process more user requests at once and increasingly complicated background operations. The **std::thread** module in C++ is useful in this situation. A simple yet powerful method to construct and manage threads, **std::thread** was introduced in C++11 and allows tasks to be completed simultaneously. Software engineers may make our application faster, more efficient, more scalable by learning how to use std::thread correctly.

Practical Solution

Creating and Using Threads

The first step in utilizing multithreading with **std::thread** involves spawning new threads and assigning them tasks to execute. Each **std::thread** instance manages a separate thread of execution. The thread starts executing immediately upon its creation, given a function (or a callable object) to run.

Following is the example of basic threading:

```
#include <iostream>

#include <thread>


// A simple function that will be executed by a thread

void printMessage(const std::string& message) {

 std::cout << "Thread message: " << message << std::endl;

}


int main() {

 // Creating a thread to execute the printMessage function

 std::thread threadObj(printMessage, "Hello from std::thread!");


 // Ensure the main thread waits for the new thread to finish

 if (threadObj.joinable()) {

 threadObj.join(); // Blocks the current thread until threadObj finishes

 }


 return 0;
```

```
}
```

In the above given sample program, **printMessage** is executed in a separate thread from the main program thread. After creating **threadObj**, the main thread waits for **threadObj** to complete its execution using **join()**. The **joinable()** check ensures that the program doesn't attempt to join a thread that's already been joined or not joinable, which would lead to a runtime error.

Managing Thread Lifecycle

It's crucial to manage the lifecycle of threads properly to avoid undefined behavior. The **join()** function is used to wait for a thread to finish its execution, ensuring that the program doesn't exit prematurely. Alternatively, **detach()** can be used to allow a thread to execute independently of the main thread, but care must be taken to ensure that detached threads do not access any resources that may be cleaned up by the main thread or become unreachable. Proper thread lifecycle management, including the use of **join()** or **detach()**, is essential to ensure that applications remain stable and resources are correctly managed.

Recipe 2: Implement Synchronization Mechanisms: Mutex, Locks, and Atomics

Situation

The importance of checking data for consistency and integrity grows as more threads run in parallel. Race conditions ill-defined behavior, or corrupted data can result from concurrent changes to shared resources that are not properly synchronized. C++ has a number of synchronization methods, such as locks, mutexes, and atomic operations, to control who has access to what shared resources. In order to create dependable programs that are thread-safe, it is essential to understand and effectively implement these principles.

Practical Solution

Mutexes and Locks

Mutexes (mutual exclusions) are used to protect shared data by only allowing one thread to access the data at a time. The **std::mutex** class offers a straightforward interface for locking and unlocking, but C++ also provides RAII-style lock management classes like **std::lock_guard** and **std::unique_lock** to simplify mutex usage and prevent common pitfalls.

Following is the example of using a mutex with **std::lock_guard**:

```
#include <iostream>
#include <mutex>
#include <thread>
#include <vector>

std::mutex mu;
int sharedData = 0;

void incrementSharedData() {
 std::lock_guard<std::mutex> lock(mu); // Locks mu upon construction and unlocks on destruction
 ++sharedData;
 std::cout << "Data incremented to " << sharedData << std::endl;
}

int main() {
 std::vector<std::thread> threads;
 for (int i = 0; i < 5; ++i) {
 threads.emplace_back(incrementSharedData);
 }

 for (auto& t : threads) {
```

```
 t.join();

 }

 return 0;

}
```

Atomic Operations

For simple data types, atomic operations offer a lock-free mechanism to ensure thread safety. C++ provides the **std::atomic** template class for types that can be read, written, or modified atomically.

Following is the example of using **std::atomic**:

```
#include <atomic>

#include <iostream>

#include <thread>

#include <vector>


std::atomic<int> atomicData(0);


void atomicIncrement() {

 int oldValue = atomicData.fetch_add(1); // Atomically increments atomicData and
returns the old value

 std::cout << "Data incremented from " << oldValue << std::endl;

}
```

```
int main() {
 std::vector<std::thread> threads;
 for (int i = 0; i < 5; ++i) {
 threads.emplace_back(atomicIncrement);
 }

 for (auto& t : threads) {
 t.join();
 }

 return 0;
}
```

Mutexes, combined with RAII-style locks, provide a robust way to protect complex data structures or sections of code that require exclusive access. For operations on simple data types, atomic operations offer a performant, lock-free alternative to ensure thread safety.

Recipe 3: Achieve Thread Safety

Situation

Thread safety is becoming increasingly important as our application adds functionality that need concurrent execution. When developing code, it is important to keep thread safety in mind. This is particularly true when dealing with shared data and numerous threads executing at the same time. Making our application thread safe will keep it efficient and dependable in all kinds of situations where there is a lot of concurrency, including when there is a race condition, a deadlock, or data corruption.

Practical Solution

Strategies for Thread Safety

Achieving thread safety in a multithreaded application like our application requires employing specific coding practices and utilizing C++ concurrency features effectively. Following are some fundamental strategies:

- Minimize Shared State: Reduce the amount of shared data accessible by multiple threads. This can involve limiting the scope of shared variables or using thread-local storage for data that does not need to be shared across threads.
- Immutable Data: Whenever possible, use immutable data structures that cannot be modified after their creation. Immutable objects are inherently thread-safe since their state cannot change, eliminating the need for synchronization.
- Synchronization Mechanisms: For data that must be shared and modified by multiple threads, use appropriate synchronization mechanisms to manage access. Mutexes, locks, and atomic operations are key tools provided by C++ for safeguarding shared resources.
- Higher-level Constructs: Leverage higher-level concurrency constructs like thread pools, futures, promises, and task-based parallelism which abstract away many low-level threading details, including some aspects of thread safety.

Following is the sample program of using Mutex for thread safety:

```
#include <iostream>

#include <mutex>

#include <thread>


std::mutex mtx; // Mutex for protecting shared data

int sharedCounter = 0;


void incrementCounter() {

 std::lock_guard<std::mutex> guard(mtx); // RAII lock management
```

```
++sharedCounter; // Critical section protected by mutex
std::cout << "Counter incremented to " << sharedCounter << std::endl;
}

int main() {
std::thread t1(incrementCounter);
std::thread t2(incrementCounter);

t1.join();
t2.join();

return 0;
}
```

In the above given sample program, a mutex is used to ensure that only one thread can modify **sharedCounter** at a time, preventing simultaneous access that could lead to incorrect results or a race condition. By adhering to the above given strategies, you can create robust, concurrent applications that are free from common pitfalls associated with multithreading. Understanding and implementing thread safety principles is essential for maintaining the integrity and performance of software in a concurrent execution environment.

Recipe 4: Explore Parallel Algorithms in C++20

Situation

When processing huge datasets like user activities or lengthy logs, our application makes use of parallel execution for operations like sorting, searching, or applying transformations. Managing threads, synchronization, and data splitting by hand is a complicated and error-prone traditional method for parallelizing these activities. The parallel algorithms in C++20 hide all of these details, so programmers can choose between sequential, parallel, or parallel plus vectorized execution based on their requirements.

Practical Solution

Leveraging Parallel Algorithms

To utilize parallel algorithms, include the header **<algorithm>** and, optionally, **<numeric>** for operations like **std::reduce**. Specify the execution policy (**std::execution::par** for parallel execution) as the first argument to the algorithm.

For example, let us perform sorting a large vector of integers significantly faster using parallel execution compared to the traditional sequential sort as below:

```
#include <algorithm>

#include <execution>

#include <vector>

#include <iostream>

#include <random>


int main() {

 std::vector<int> data(1000000);

 std::iota(data.begin(), data.end(), 1); // Fill with sequential numbers

 std::shuffle(data.begin(), data.end(), std::mt19937{std::random_device{}()}); // Shuffle
data


 // Sort data in parallel

 std::sort(std::execution::par, data.begin(), data.end());
```

```
std::cout << "Data sorted in parallel." << std::endl;


return 0;

}
```

Choosing the Right Execution Policy

- Sequential (default): **std::execution::seq** for operations that must be performed sequentially.
- Parallel: **std::execution::par** allows the implementation to parallelize the algorithm.
- Parallel and Vectorized: **std::execution::par_unseq** suggests that parallel execution and vectorization optimizations are permissible, potentially offering the highest performance for suitable algorithms and hardware.

By simply specifying an execution policy, our application can leverage parallelism in standard algorithms, making operations on large datasets more efficient. It's essential to profile and test the performance implications of different execution policies, as the optimal choice can vary based on the algorithm, data size, and hardware capabilities.

Recipe 5: Manage Thread Lifecycle and State

Situation

In order to enhance performance or responsiveness, several procedures could be executed concurrently. But, issues might arise when threads are created and managed carelessly. For example, threads could remain operating in the background if an application is exited too soon, or race situations could occur if thread execution was not properly synchronized. Building reliable and performant applications requires you to have a firm grasp of thread management concepts including starting, synchronizing, and stopping.

Practical Solution

Starting Threads

Threads in C++ are started by creating an instance of **std::thread**, passing a function (or callable object) to run in the thread.

```
#include <thread>

#include <iostream>


void doWork() {

 std::cout << "Thread is doing work\n";

}


int main() {

 std::thread worker(doWork);


 // Ensure main waits for worker to finish

 if (worker.joinable()) {

 worker.join();

 }


 return 0;

}
```

Thread Synchronization

Synchronizing threads is essential to ensure that they execute in the correct order or manage access to shared resources safely.

- Using **std::mutex** for Resource Access: Protect shared data using mutexes, locking them before access and unlocking after.

- Condition Variables for Coordination: Use **std::condition_variable** along with **std::mutex** to wait for or signal specific conditions between threads.

Stopping Threads Gracefully

Threads should not be forcibly terminated; instead, they should complete their work and exit naturally. Use flags or condition variables to signal a thread to stop.

```
#include <atomic>

#include <chrono>


std::atomic<bool> shouldStop(false);


void workUntilSignaled() {

 while (!shouldStop.load()) {

 // Perform work...

 std::this_thread::sleep_for(std::chrono::milliseconds(100)); // Simulate work

 }

 std::cout << "Thread stopping as signaled.\n";

}
```

Managing Thread State

- Joining Threads: Always **join** or **detach** threads before they go out of scope to avoid terminating the program unexpectedly.
- Detaching Threads: If a thread should run independently of the thread that spawned it, **detach** it, but ensure its resources are managed appropriately.

Engineers working on "GitforGits" can take advantage of concurrency to boost application performance without falling into the typical traps of multithreaded programming by meticulously initiating, synchronizing, and terminating threads. Ensuring data integrity and coordinating thread execution are made possible by proper synchronization methods, which include mutexes and condition variables. To keep applications healthy and stop resource leaks, it is essential to gracefully end threads and manage their state effectively.

Recipe 6: Concurrency with Futures and Promises

Situation

To keep the user interface responsive and the execution fast, it is necessary to handle asynchronous operations. These operations may include retrieving data from a server or running a long-running computation. C++ offers **std::future** and **std::promise** as part of its concurrency library to facilitate these operations. **std::future** provides a mechanism to access the result of asynchronous operations, while **std::promise** is a way to set the value of a **future**. Understanding how to effectively use these constructs allows you to manage asynchronous tasks more robustly and cleanly.

Practical Solution

Using std::promise and std::future

std::promise and **std::future** work together to communicate data between threads. A **promise** is used to set a value or an exception that can be retrieved later by a **future**. This pattern is particularly useful when you need to asynchronously execute a task and retrieve its result in the future.

Following is the example demonstrating **std::promise** and **std::future**:

```
#include <iostream>

#include <future>

#include <thread>



void fetchDataFromDB(std::promise<std::string> &&promise) {

 std::this_thread::sleep_for(std::chrono::seconds(2)); // Simulate work

 promise.set_value("DB_Result");
```

```
}


int main() {
 // Create a promise
 std::promise<std::string> promise;


 // Fetch the future from the promise
 std::future<std::string> future = promise.get_future();


 // Start a thread and move the promise into it
 std::thread dbThread(fetchDataFromDB, std::move(promise));


 // Do other work in the meantime
 std::cout << "Fetching data from DB" << std::endl;


 // Wait for the result and retrieve it
 std::string dbResult = future.get();


 // Output the result
 std::cout << "Data received: " << dbResult << std::endl;
```

```
// Clean up the thread

dbThread.join();



return 0;

}
```

In the above given sample program, a separate thread is spawned to simulate fetching data from a database. The **promise** object is used within this thread to set the result of the operation, which is then retrieved by the main thread through a **future**.

Benefits of std::future and std::promise

- Synchronization and Communication: They provide a built-in mechanism for communicating results between threads, simplifying synchronization.
- Error Handling: **std::future** can store exceptions raised in the worker thread, which can then be rethrown in the thread calling **future.get()**, facilitating error handling across thread boundaries.
- Blocking and Non-blocking Operations: **future.get()** blocks until the result is available, while **future.wait()** and **future.wait_for()** allow for non-blocking waits, offering flexibility in managing asynchronous tasks.

std::future and **std::promise** are powerful tools for managing asynchronous operations in C++ applications like our application. They simplify the task of executing work in background threads and retrieving the results in a thread-safe manner.

Recipe 7: Implement Task-based Concurrency

Situation

Using task-based concurrency becomes critical for efficiently handling the application's increasing burden. This method streamlines the administration of concurrent operations by directing attention away from the nitty-gritty of threading and onto the tasks you wish to do in parallel. To help with this, C++ introduced std::async, std::future, and the task-based programming model, which allow you to build asynchronous code that is clean and easy to maintain. To significantly enhance the application's responsiveness and throughput, task-based concurrency is highly beneficial for processes that may be executed in parallel, such handling user requests or running background calculations.

Practical Solution

Using std::async for Task-based Concurrency

std::async runs a function asynchronously (potentially in a new thread) and returns a **std::future** that will eventually hold the result of that function. This mechanism is ideal for executing tasks that are independent and can be processed in parallel.

Following is the example of task-based concurrency with **std::async**:

```
#include <iostream>

#include <vector>

#include <future>


int performComputation(int data) {

 // Simulate a computation

 return data * data;

}


int main() {

 std::vector<std::future<int>> futures;


 // Launch multiple tasks asynchronously

 for (int i = 0; i < 10; ++i) {

 futures.push_back(std::async(std::launch::async, performComputation, i));

 }
```

```
// Retrieve and print the results of the computations
for (auto& future : futures) {
std::cout << "Result: " << future.get() << std::endl;
}


return 0;
}
```

In the above given sample program, **std::async** is used to launch several tasks that compute the square of a number. Each call to **std::async** returns a **std::future**, which is used to retrieve the result of the computation once it's completed. The **std::launch::async** policy argument specifies that each task should be run asynchronously in its own thread.

Benefits of Task-based Concurrency

- Simplicity and Flexibility: The task-based model abstracts away the complexities of thread management, focusing on what needs to be done rather than how it's executed concurrently.
- Improved Scalability: By allowing the system to manage task execution, applications can scale more effectively across processors.
- Enhanced Responsiveness: Splitting work into tasks that can be executed in parallel can significantly reduce execution time for CPU-bound operations or I/O latency.

Recipe 8: Avoid Deadlocks

Situation

A deadlock could occur in our program because of the number of threads that use common data structures or input/output devices. Consider two threads, one of which needs resources A and B in order to continue, and the other of which needs resources B and A in order to continue. It is possible for threads to become stuck waiting for each other forever if they lock the first resource before trying to lock the second.

Practical Solution

Multithreaded programs including our application rely on avoiding deadlocks to keep running smoothly and responsive. When many threads cannot move forward because they are all waiting for the other thread to release a resource that they require, this situation is called a deadlock. Your application's performance and reliability could take a major hit in this scenario. Developers working with concurrent systems must possess the ability to recognize possible deadlocks and implement techniques to prevent them.

Lock Ordering

A common strategy to avoid deadlocks is to enforce a consistent order in which locks are acquired. If all threads lock resources in the same order, circular wait conditions (one of the necessary conditions for deadlocks) can be prevented.

Following is the sample program:

```
std::mutex mutexA, mutexB;


void thread1Function() {

 std::lock_guard<std::mutex> lockA(mutexA); // First lock A

 // Perform some operation...

 std::lock_guard<std::mutex> lockB(mutexB); // Then lock B

 // Perform operations involving A and B

}


void thread2Function() {

 std::lock_guard<std::mutex> lockA(mutexA); // First lock A, as in thread1Function

 // Perform some operation...

 std::lock_guard<std::mutex> lockB(mutexB); // Then lock B, maintaining the order
```

```
 // Perform operations involving A and B
}
```

By ensuring both threads lock **mutexA** and **mutexB** in the same order, the deadlock scenario is avoided.

Lock Granularity

Reducing the scope and duration of locks (making them as fine-grained as possible) can also help prevent deadlocks by minimizing the window in which locks can interfere with each other.

Use of **std::lock** *for Multiple Locks*

When acquiring multiple locks at once, **std::lock** can be used to lock all at once without risking deadlock. It employs a deadlock avoidance algorithm (typically try-lock) to ensure that all locks are acquired before proceeding.

Following is the sample program:

```
void processResources() {
 std::lock(mutexA, mutexB); // Lock both mutexes without deadlock risk
 std::lock_guard<std::mutex> lockA(mutexA, std::adopt_lock);
 std::lock_guard<std::mutex> lockB(mutexB, std::adopt_lock);
 // Perform operations involving resources protected by mutexA and mutexB
}
```

Ensure that a thread does not hold onto locks while waiting for other resources or operations that might cause other threads to wait.

Strategies like enforcing a consistent lock ordering, reducing lock granularity, utilizing **std::lock** for acquiring multiple locks, and being mindful of holding locks during waits, are effective in preventing deadlocks. Additionally, employing tools and techniques for dynamic deadlock detection can help identify and resolve deadlock scenarios during the development and testing phases.

Summary

In this chapter, we learned all about C++'s parallel execution features, which helped us understand how to use concurrent programming to its maximum potential and implement solutions. The chapter began with an introduction to threading using std::thread and continued with instructions on how to create, manage, and synchronize threads such that they may complete tasks simultaneously. This laid the groundwork for more advanced multithreaded systems. We learned about atomics, mutexes, and locks as synchronization mechanisms, and how important it is to control who has access to shared resources. This helped us understand how to avoid race scenarios and ensure data is intact in "GitforGits."

The std::async function, futures, and promises were utilized in the task-based parallelism trip through concurrency, which helped to simplify asynchronous programming and manage task lifecycles and state effectively. Thanks to new opportunities presented by C++20's parallel algorithms, our application was able to drastically enhance performance with almost no code modifications when processing data. In addition, the chapter covered important topics related to concurrent programming, such as thread safety, error handling policy design, and deadlock avoidance. Building strong, efficient, and scalable applications requires meticulous planning and following concurrency best practices, as discussed in these topics. By utilizing these sophisticated features, you can overcome the obstacles of concurrent programming. This will allow our application to make better use of the available computational resources, which will improve its performance and user experience.

CHAPTER 8: PERFORMANCE AND MEMORY MANAGEMENT

Introduction

This chapter focuses on the key components of improving the speed of C++ application execution and efficiently managing resources. For optimal memory usage and execution performance, this chapter dives into advanced techniques and best practices. With these optimizations, the application will run efficiently and scale well under heavy load. Beginning with an examination of RAII (Resource Acquisition Is Initialization) and resource management, we lay the groundwork for automatic and secure resource management, which minimizes memory leaks and guarantees correct release of resources when they are no longer needed.

Smart pointers, such as std::shared_ptr, std::weak_ptr, and std::unique_ptr, are extensively covered in the following section of the chapter. To automate life cycle management of dynamic memory, lessen the burden of manual memory management, and minimize errors, these tools are crucial in modern C++. We also investigate methods for managing memory that you can create specifically for your applications, which could lead to better memory utilization and overall performance.

This chapter also goes over ways to make C++ apps run faster by optimizing algorithms, learning about and lowering time complexity, and finding bottlenecks with profiling tools. To improve memory usage patterns, we learn about memory pools and efficient allocation strategies. This is particularly true in situations where objects of the same size are allocated and deallocated often. Lastly, we delve into C++ coding practices that are cache-friendly, with an emphasis on data locality and access patterns that correspond to the hardware's cache design for optimal execution speed. These subjects provide you with the know-how and resources you need to create memory-efficient, high-performance apps that can keep up with the demands of today's software ecosystems.

Recipe 1: Explore RAII and Resource Management

Situation

It is critical to manage resources such as memory, file handles, and network connections efficiently to ensure the reliability and performance of applications. A key component of efficient resource management in C++ is the RAII paradigm, which guarantees correct acquisition and release of resources. To keep errors and leaks to a minimum, RAII uses object lifetimes and constructor/destructor behavior for resource management.

Practical Solution

Understanding RAII

RAII is a design pattern that binds the lifecycle of a resource (such as dynamically allocated memory or a file handle) to the lifetime of an object. A resource is acquired during an object's creation (typically in its constructor) and released during the object's destruction (in its destructor). This pattern ensures that resources are always released appropriately, even in the face of exceptions, since destructors are called automatically when objects go out of scope.

Practical Implementation

Creating a simple RAII wrapper for a file handle demonstrates how RAII can manage resources:

```
#include <iostream>

#include <fstream>

#include <string>


class FileHandle {

 std::fstream file;


public:

 FileHandle(const std::string& filename, std::ios_base::openmode mode =
std::ios_base::in | std::ios_base::out) {

 file.open(filename, mode);

 if (!file.is_open()) {

 throw std::runtime_error("Failed to open file");

 }

 }


 ~FileHandle() {
```

```
file.close(); // Ensure file is always closed when the FileHandle object is destroyed
}

// Disable copy operations to ensure unique ownership of the resource
FileHandle(const FileHandle&) = delete;
FileHandle& operator=(const FileHandle&) = delete;

// Enable move operations for transfer of ownership
FileHandle(FileHandle&& other) noexcept : file(std::move(other.file)) {}
FileHandle& operator=(FileHandle&& other) noexcept {
file = std::move(other.file);
return *this;
}

std::fstream& get() { return file; }
};

void useFile(const std::string& path) {
FileHandle fileHandle(path); // File is opened
// Use the file
fileHandle.get() << "Hello, RAII!" << std::endl;
```

```
// File is automatically closed when fileHandle goes out of scope
}


int main() {
 try {
 useFile("example.txt");
 } catch (const std::exception& e) {
 std::cerr << e.what() << std::endl;
 }
 return 0;
}
```

The above sample program illustrates how RAII can be used to manage a file resource. The **FileHandle** class automatically opens the file upon construction and closes it upon destruction, ensuring the file is never left open accidentally. By leveraging RAII, you can write safer, cleaner resource management code.

Advantages of RAII

- Exception Safety: RAII provides strong guarantees against resource leaks, especially in the presence of exceptions. Resources are always cleaned up correctly, as destructors are invoked automatically by the C++ runtime.
- Simplicity: Code that uses RAII is often simpler and more straightforward, as it eliminates the need for explicit clean-up code scattered throughout the application.
- Resource Ownership and Lifetimes: RAII clarifies resource ownership and lifecycle management, making it easier to reason about the program's behavior.

In addition to preventing resource leaks, RAII improves code safety and maintainability by automatically releasing resources when they are no longer needed.

Recipe 2: Using std::unique_ptr

Situation

Managing dynamic memory efficiently and safely is crucial for building robust applications. **std::unique_ptr** is a smart pointer provided by the C++ Standard Library that facilitates automatic memory management, ensuring that dynamically allocated memory is deleted when no longer needed. It encapsulates a raw pointer and takes sole ownership of the memory it points to, making it an excellent tool for resource management in "GitforGits."

Ownership and Lifecycle

std::unique_ptr owns the memory it points to exclusively. When the **std::unique_ptr** goes out of scope, its destructor is called, and the memory is automatically deallocated. This ownership model prevents memory leaks and makes **std::unique_ptr** ideal for managing resources in an RAII fashion.

Creating and Using std::unique_ptr

std::unique_ptr can be created using the **std::make_unique** function introduced in C++14, which allocates memory for the managed object and returns a **std::unique_ptr** to it.

```
#include <memory>

#include <iostream>



class Resource {

public:

 Resource() { std::cout << "Resource acquired\n"; }

 ~Resource() { std::cout << "Resource released\n"; }

 void doSomething() { std::cout << "Doing something\n"; }

};
```

```
void useResource() {

 auto ptr = std::make_unique<Resource>();

 ptr->doSomething();

 // No need to manually delete the pointer; memory is automatically freed when ptr goes out of scope

}



int main() {

 useResource();

 return 0;

}
```

Transfer of Ownership

std::unique_ptr cannot be copied, ensuring unique ownership of the resource. However, ownership can be transferred using **std::move**, making it possible to return a **std::unique_ptr** from a function or pass it to another function.

```
std::unique_ptr<Resource> createResource() {

 return std::make_unique<Resource>();

}



void consumeResource(std::unique_ptr<Resource> res) {

 res->doSomething();

}
```

```
int main() {
 auto res = createResource();
 consumeResource(std::move(res));
 // res is now nullptr; ownership has been transferred to consumeResource
 return 0;
}
```

Benefits

- Automatic Memory Management: Ensures resources are properly released when no longer needed, preventing memory leaks.
- Exception Safety: Provides strong guarantees, especially in the presence of exceptions, by ensuring resources are cleaned up.
- Explicit Ownership Semantics: Makes it clear who owns a particular resource at any point in the code, improving readability and maintainability.

std::unique_ptr simplifies dynamic memory management, making code safer, cleaner, and more maintainable. Its strict ownership model and automatic resource cleanup capabilities make it an essential component for modern C++ applications, including "GitforGits."

Recipe 3: Using std::shared_ptr

Situation

std::shared_ptr is a type of smart pointer provided by the C++ Standard Library that manages a dynamically allocated object through a shared ownership model. Multiple **std::shared_ptr** instances can own the same object, and the managed object is destroyed automatically once the last **shared_ptr** owning it is destroyed or reset. This feature makes **std::shared_ptr** ideal for use cases in our application where objects are accessed by multiple owners or parts of the program.

Shared Ownership

The fundamental characteristic of **std::shared_ptr** is its ability to share ownership of an object. This shared ownership ensures that the object remains alive as long as there is at least one

std::shared_ptr instance pointing to it. The memory is deallocated when the reference count drops to zero, which happens when the last **shared_ptr** pointing to the object is destroyed or assigned a new object.

Creating and Using std::shared_ptr

A **std::shared_ptr** can be created using the **std::make_shared** function, which allocates the object and returns a **std::shared_ptr** that owns it. **std::make_shared** is preferred over direct use of the **std::shared_ptr** constructor because it performs a single allocation for both the object and its control block, improving performance.

```
#include <memory>

#include <iostream>

#include <vector>


class Widget {

public:

 Widget() { std::cout << "Widget constructed\n"; }

 ~Widget() { std::cout << "Widget destroyed\n"; }

 void display() const { std::cout << "Displaying Widget\n"; }

};


void processWidgets(std::shared_ptr<Widget> widget) {

 widget->display();

 // The widget is not destroyed here, as the ownership is shared

}
```

```
int main() {
 auto widget = std::make_shared<Widget>();
 processWidgets(widget);
 // Widget is destroyed automatically when the last shared_ptr (widget) is out of scope
 return 0;
}
```

Reference Counting

std::shared_ptr uses reference counting to keep track of how many **shared_ptr** instances own the same object. This count is incremented when a new **shared_ptr** is copied from another that owns the object and decremented when a **shared_ptr** is destroyed or reset.

Cyclic References

One potential pitfall of **std::shared_ptr** is the possibility of cyclic references, where two or more objects owned by **std::shared_ptr** instances refer to each other, preventing their destruction. To break such cycles, **std::weak_ptr** can be used for back-references or in situations where an owning relationship is not required.

Benefits

- Automatic Resource Management: Ensures proper resource cleanup, reducing the risk of memory leaks.
- Shared Ownership Semantics: Facilitates scenarios where objects need to be accessed by multiple parts of a program without strict ownership hierarchy.
- Thread Safety: Operations on **std::shared_ptr** itself (copying, assignment, destruction) are thread-safe with respect to other operations on the same **std::shared_ptr** object.

Recipe 4: Using std::weak_ptr

Situation

std::weak_ptr is a smart pointer provided by the C++ Standard Library that complements **std::shared_ptr** by holding a non-owning ("weak") reference to an object that is managed by **std::shared_ptr**. This mechanism is crucial for breaking cyclic dependencies among shared objects, which can lead to memory leaks since the reference count never reaches zero. Understanding how to use **std::weak_ptr** effectively is essential for managing complex relationships in applications like our application without compromising memory management.

Breaking Cycles with std::weak_ptr

std::weak_ptr is designed to break cyclic references. When two or more objects refer to each other with **std::shared_ptr**, they keep each other alive indefinitely, creating a memory leak. **std::weak_ptr** allows one side of the relationship to be a weak link, not contributing to the reference count, thereby allowing objects to be destroyed properly.

Creating and Using std::weak_ptr

A **std::weak_ptr** is typically created from a **std::shared_ptr**, pointing to the same object without increasing its reference count. To access the object, a **std::weak_ptr** must be converted to a **std::shared_ptr** using the **lock** method, which checks whether the object exists and, if so, returns a valid **std::shared_ptr** to it.

Consider a scenario where users can have mutual followers, potentially creating cyclic references if not handled correctly.

```
#include <iostream>

#include <memory>

#include <vector>



class User;

using UserPtr = std::shared_ptr<User>;

using WeakUserPtr = std::weak_ptr<User>;



class User {

 std::string name;

 std::vector<WeakUserPtr> followers; // Use std::weak_ptr to avoid cyclic references

public:
```

```
User(const std::string& name) : name(name) {}
~User() { std::cout << "User " << name << " destroyed\n"; }

void addFollower(UserPtr follower) {
followers.push_back(WeakUserPtr(follower));
}

void displayFollowers() {
std::cout << "Followers of " << name << ":\n";
for (const auto& weakFollower : followers) {
if (auto follower = weakFollower.lock()) { // Convert to shared_ptr to use
std::cout << "- " << follower->name << "\n";
}
}
}
};

int main() {
auto alice = std::make_shared<User>("Alice");
auto bob = std::make_shared<User>("Bob");
```

```
alice->addFollower(bob);

bob->addFollower(alice); // Without weak_ptr, this would create a cyclic reference



alice->displayFollowers();

bob->displayFollowers();



return 0;

}
```

In the above given sample program, users Alice and Bob follow each other. By using **std::weak_ptr** for the follower list, we prevent cyclic references, allowing both User objects to be destroyed properly when their shared pointers go out of scope.

Benefits

- Memory Leak Prevention: Effectively breaks cyclic references among shared objects.
- Flexibility: Offers a safe way to access an object that might be deleted by another owner.
- Usage Safety: **std::weak_ptr** provides a mechanism (**lock**) to verify the existence of the object before accessing it, enhancing program safety.

std::weak_ptr provides solutions to cyclic references and memory management challenges in complex object graphs. It allows for the construction of more sophisticated data structures and relationships in C++ applications without the risk of memory leaks.

Recipe 5: Implement Custom Memory Management Technique

Situation

The standard memory allocation (e.g., **new** and **delete** in C++) can be inefficient for applications that frequently allocate and deallocate small objects due to overhead and fragmentation. A custom memory allocator can mitigate these issues by providing more control over how memory is allocated, reused, and released, often by batching allocations, maintaining pools of reusable objects, or aligning memory allocations to cache lines.

Practical Solution

"GitforGits" requires the rapid allocation and deallocation of numerous small objects representing user actions or messages. A custom memory pool allocator can significantly reduce allocation overhead and fragmentation compared to the default allocator.

Implementing a Simple Memory Pool

A memory pool allocates a large block of memory upfront and divides it into smaller chunks that are managed internally, providing a fast path for allocation and deallocation by avoiding system calls.

Following is a sample program:

```
#include <iostream>

#include <vector>

#include <cassert>



class PoolAllocator {

 struct FreeNode {

 FreeNode* next;

 };



 FreeNode* freeList = nullptr;

 void* poolStart = nullptr;

 size_t chunkSize;

 size_t poolSize;
```

```
public:
 PoolAllocator(size_t chunkSize, size_t numChunks) : chunkSize(chunkSize),
poolSize(chunkSize * numChunks) {
 poolStart = operator new(poolSize);
 freeList = static_cast<FreeNode*>(poolStart);

 FreeNode* current = freeList;
 for (size_t i = 1; i < numChunks; ++i) {
 current->next = reinterpret_cast<FreeNode*>(reinterpret_cast<char*>(poolStart) + i
* chunkSize);
 current = current->next;
 }
 current->next = nullptr;
 }

 void* allocate() {
 if (!freeList) {
 throw std::bad_alloc();
 }
 FreeNode* allocated = freeList;
 freeList = freeList->next;
 return allocated;
```

```
}

void deallocate(void* pointer) {
FreeNode* node = static_cast<FreeNode*>(pointer);
node->next = freeList;
freeList = node;
}

~PoolAllocator() {
operator delete(poolStart);
}

// Prevent copying and assignment
PoolAllocator(const PoolAllocator&) = delete;
PoolAllocator& operator=(const PoolAllocator&) = delete;
};

// Usage example with a dummy object
class MyObject {
// Object data members
public:
```

```
void* operator new(size_t size, PoolAllocator& pool) {
return pool.allocate();
}
void operator delete(void* pointer, size_t size) {
// In a real scenario, we'd need a way to access the corresponding pool here
}
};

int main() {
PoolAllocator pool(sizeof(MyObject), 100); // Pool for 100 MyObject instances


MyObject* obj = new (pool) MyObject(); // Allocate an object from the pool
// Use the object


delete obj; // Deallocate the object, returning it to the pool
return 0;
}
```

This simplistic example shows how to manage allocations of a fixed-size object using a basic memory pool allocator. By managing individual allocations from a large block of memory that has already been pre-allocated, it drastically reduces the overhead of frequent allocations and deallocations. Custom allocators can improve scalability and execution speed by reducing overhead and fragmentation and making better use of system resources.

Recipe 6: Optimize Speed in C++ Applications

Situation

Improving the performance of C++ programs calls for a holistic strategy that takes into account both the code and its interactions with the hardware. Performance optimization is of the utmost importance for "GitforGits," which may handle massive amounts of data or necessitate responsiveness in real-time. Methods for optimizing algorithms, coding efficiently, and making the most of hardware capabilities are all covered in this recipe with an eye toward increasing execution speed.

Practical Solution

Analyzing Performance Bottlenecks

Begin with profiling to identify bottlenecks. Tools like gprof, Valgrind's Callgrind, or Visual Studio's Profiler can help pinpoint where your application spends most of its time or consumes excessive resources. Focus on optimizing these critical sections first.

Algorithm Optimization

Often, the choice of algorithm or data structure can have a significant impact on performance. For example, using hash maps (**std::unordered_map**) for frequent lookup operations instead of a vector (**std::vector**) can drastically reduce search times from O(n) to O(1) on average. And, look for opportunities to eliminate redundant calculations, cache results of expensive operations, and early exit from loops when possible.

Code Optimization Techniques

- Function Inlining: Use **inline** keyword for small, frequently called functions to eliminate the overhead of function calls. However, rely on the compiler's judgment where possible, as modern compilers are quite good at deciding when to inline.
- Loop Unrolling: Manually or using compiler pragmas, loop unrolling can reduce loop overhead for tight loops. Be mindful of code readability and size.
- Minimize Copying: Use move semantics where applicable and consider passing objects by reference or using **std::move** to avoid unnecessary copies of large objects.

Memory Access Patterns

- Reduce Cache Misses: Structure data and access patterns to maximize cache efficiency. For example, accessing memory sequentially rather than randomly can significantly speed up operations due to the way modern CPUs cache data.

- Data Locality: Keep related data close together in memory if they are accessed together, taking advantage of spatial locality.

Leverage Parallelism

- Multithreading and Asynchronous Programming: Utilize **std::async**, **std::thread**, or higher-level abstractions like thread pools to parallelize work across multiple cores.
- Vectorization: Use SIMD (Single Instruction, Multiple Data) instructions where possible, either via compiler auto-vectorization or through explicit use of intrinsics.

So, we must pretend that our application handles a very big dataset. Processing of data is initially carried out in a sequential fashion. This is identified as a bottleneck through profiling. Processing time is drastically decreased by utilizing a parallel algorithm:

```
#include <algorithm>

#include <vector>

#include <execution>


void processData(std::vector<int>& data) {

 // Assume process() is a CPU-intensive operation

 std::transform(std::execution::par, data.begin(), data.end(), data.begin(), [](int val) {

 return process(val);

 });

}
```

Using **std::execution::par** tells the compiler to execute the **std::transform** algorithm in parallel, automatically distributing the work across available CPU cores.

Continual Testing and Profiling

Performance optimization is an iterative process. Each change should be followed by testing to ensure it has the desired effect and doesn't introduce new issues. Keep profiling periodically as your application evolves.

A holistic strategy is needed to optimize C++ application speed, taking into account not only algorithmic efficiency but also the application's memory access patterns, parallel execution capabilities, and the underlying hardware. You can significantly improve the performance of GitforGits by concentrating on important sections identified through profiling, utilizing efficient algorithms and data structures, optimizing code, and making use of hardware capabilities. Optimization involves finding a balance between performance, readability, maintainability, and development time.

Recipe 7: Manage Memory Pools and Efficient Allocation

Situation

The performance of C++ applications, that require real-time processing or have high throughput demands, can be significantly improved with efficient allocation strategies and memory pool management. To improve cache locality and minimize fragmentation of our application, memory pools pre-allocate large blocks of memory and serve individual allocations from these blocks. This significantly reduces the overhead of dynamic memory allocation and deallocation.

Practical Solution

Understanding Memory Pools

Memory pools allocate a large block of memory upfront, which is then divided into smaller, fixed-size chunks. These chunks are managed internally within the pool and can be quickly allocated and deallocated to and from the application, bypassing the more costly operations of the standard memory allocator.

Benefits of Memory Pools

- Reduced Allocation Overhead: By avoiding frequent calls to the system's memory allocator, memory pools decrease the time spent in memory allocation and deallocation.
- Improved Cache Locality: Memory pools often improve cache locality by allocating objects that are frequently accessed together from the same block of memory.
- Minimized Fragmentation: Allocating fixed-size blocks reduces fragmentation, ensuring more predictable performance and efficient use of memory.

Designing a Memory Pool

A simple memory pool for objects of a single size can be implemented by keeping a linked list of free blocks. When an object is allocated, a block is removed from the free list. When an object is deallocated, its block is returned to the free list.

Following is the sample program:

```
class MemoryPool {
 struct Block {
 Block* next;
 };

 Block* freeList = nullptr;
 size_t blockSize;
 size_t blockCount;

 void expandPoolSize() {
 size_t size = blockSize + sizeof(Block*);
 Block* block = reinterpret_cast<Block*>(new char[size]);
 block->next = freeList;
 freeList = block;
 }

public:
 MemoryPool(size_t blockSize, size_t initialCount) : blockSize(blockSize),
blockCount(initialCount) {
 for (size_t i = 0; i < initialCount; ++i) {
```

```
expandPoolSize();
}
}

void* allocate() {
if (!freeList) {
expandPoolSize();
}
Block* block = freeList;
freeList = block->next;
return reinterpret_cast<void*>(++block);
}

void deallocate(void* pointer) {
Block* block = reinterpret_cast<Block*>(pointer);
--block;
block->next = freeList;
freeList = block;
}

~MemoryPool() {
```

```
while (freeList) {
Block* next = freeList->next;
delete[] reinterpret_cast<char*>(freeList);
freeList = next;
}
}
};
```

The above sample program outlines a basic memory pool that manages a pool of blocks. It expands the pool by adding new blocks when needed and maintains a linked list of free blocks for allocation. The destructor ensures cleanup of all allocated blocks. Do remember that implementing a custom memory pool requires careful consideration of the application's needs and thorough testing.

Recipe 8: Perform Cache-Friendly C++ Coding

Situation

When writing high-performance C++, optimizing code for cache utilization is essential. Caches in modern CPUs are multi-tiered and much quicker than main memory access. By minimizing the frequency of cache misses—which happen when computation-related data is not present in the cache and must be retrieved from slower memory—efficient cache utilization can significantly boost application performance. In this recipe, we will look at ways to make C++ code that is cache-friendly by reducing cache misses and making data local as much as possible.

Practical Solution

Understanding Cache Usage

A CPU cache stores a small amount of memory close to the processor to speed up the access to frequently used data.

The principle of locality is:

- Temporal Locality: The tendency of a processor to access the same memory locations repeatedly over a short period.

- Spatial Locality: The tendency of a processor to access memory locations that are close to those it has recently accessed.

Strategies for Cache-Friendly Code

- Data Structure Alignment and Padding: Ensure that data structures are aligned to cache line boundaries and consider padding them to avoid false sharing in multithreading scenarios. False sharing occurs when multiple threads modify variables that, although independent, reside on the same cache line, leading to unnecessary cache invalidation and reduced performance.

- Sequential Memory Access: Access memory sequentially rather than randomly. Sequential access patterns are more predictable and allow the prefetching mechanisms of modern CPUs to load data into cache proactively.

- Minimize Memory Footprint: Use compact data structures and minimize the size of hot data. Smaller data structures that fit within a cache line are accessed more quickly, reducing cache misses.

- Loop Nesting and Iteration Order: Consider the memory layout of multi-dimensional arrays or data structures when nesting loops. Access data in an order that corresponds to its layout in memory to improve spatial locality.

Pretend for a second that our application is dealing with a huge matrix, or 2D array. The data is stored in memory in a specific way, so accessing the matrix row-wise instead of column-wise can significantly impact performance.

```
constexpr size_t SIZE = 1024;

int matrix[SIZE][SIZE];



// Row-wise access (Cache-friendly)

for(size_t i = 0; i < SIZE; ++i) {

 for(size_t j = 0; j < SIZE; ++j) {

 matrix[i][j] *= 2;

 }

}
```

```
// Column-wise access (Less cache-friendly)
for(size_t j = 0; j < SIZE; ++j) {
 for(size_t i = 0; i < SIZE; ++i) {
 matrix[i][j] *= 2;
 }
}
```

Because it follows the order in which the array is stored in memory, row-wise access is better for the cache in this case. Cache misses are more common with column-wise access because it skips over memory pages. Optimization of loop iteration orders, data structure alignment, sequential memory access, and reducing the memory footprint of hot data are effective strategies to improve cache utilization and achieve significant speedups.

Summary

This chapter explored advanced methods for improving the performance of C++ programs, with an emphasis on making better use of memory and running the code faster. The chapter began with an exploration of RAII and smart pointers (**std::unique_ptr**, **shared_ptr**, **weak_ptr**), foundational concepts for managing resources automatically and safely. These tools mitigate common issues such as memory leaks and dangling pointers, underpinning robust application architecture in "GitforGits." Enhanced performance through reduced overhead and better control over memory layout and allocation patterns can be achieved through the use of custom memory management techniques, which were discussed in detail. These techniques can be applied in situations where default memory allocation strategies do not adequately address the problem.

Methods for improving application performance, such as using cache-friendly code and optimizing algorithms, became clear as the story developed. When dealing with dynamic memory in high-performance settings, it became clear that efficient allocation techniques and pool management were crucial for reducing fragmentation and allocation costs. The importance of knowing hardware details, like cache architecture, in creating efficient code was highlighted by the investigation of cache-friendly coding. Achieving substantial speed improvements, our application reduces cache misses and maximizes the CPU's caching mechanism by accessing data in patterns that match cache design. The focus on careful and informed memory and performance management throughout this chapter provided a thorough overview of the resources available to you for creating efficient and high-performing C++ applications.

CHAPTER 9: ADVANCED TYPE MANIPULATION

Introduction

Through type manipulation and compile-time knowledge, C++ developers can construct more generic, efficient, and adaptable programs. In order to better handle the complicated programming problems that arise in the "GitforGits" application, this chapter will teach you how to fully utilize C++'s type system.

Sophisticated methods for dynamic type management, speed optimization, and code reuse are essential for modern C++ programs. You can design code that elegantly handles type-related decisions, computes at compile time, and adapts to new types automatically if they understand and implement advanced type manipulation techniques.

This chapter will cover following recipes:

- Explore Type Traits and Type Utilities: We will start by exploring type traits and utilities provided by the C++ Standard Library, which offer a way to query and manipulate type information at compile time. This foundational knowledge is crucial for writing generic and type-safe code.
- Use Custom Type Traits: Beyond the standard type traits, creating custom type traits allows for expressing complex type constraints and behaviors specific to your application's needs, enabling more expressive and adaptable templates.
- Implement SFINAE Technique: The SFINAE (Substitution Failure Is Not An Error) principle is a cornerstone of template metaprogramming, allowing for the selection of different function or class template specializations based on the types used.
- Template Metaprogramming: We will dive into template metaprogramming techniques, enabling computations and logic to be executed at compile time, leading to highly optimized runtime code.
- Using **constexpr** for Compile-Time Calculations: The **constexpr** specifier will be explored to define expressions, functions, and even constructors that can be evaluated at compile time, further enhancing performance.
- Advanced Use of **decltype**: We will cover how to use **decltype** for type deduction in complex expressions and scenarios, improving code generality and flexibility.
- Implement Custom Compile-Time Functions: Building on **constexpr**, we will implement custom functions that execute at compile time, enabling sophisticated compile-time logic and calculations.
- Implement Type Erasure Technique: Finally, type erasure techniques will be discussed as a way to abstract away type information, enabling operations on different types through a common interface, increasing runtime flexibility without sacrificing type safety.

These recipes provide an in-depth look at the inner workings of C++ type manipulation, teaching you sophisticated techniques that make code more efficient, robust, and easy to maintain.

Recipe 1: Explore Type Traits and Type Utilities

Situation

It is incredibly important to fully understand and make use of the capabilities of type utilities and type attributes when designing sophisticated features. The C++ Standard Library provides several tools for inspecting and manipulating type information during compilation. The foundation for complex type manipulation lies in type characteristics and utilities, which are used for optimizing template code, guaranteeing type safety, and implementing generic programming approaches.

Practical Solution

Understanding Type Traits

Type traits in C++ are templates that provide a standardized way to query characteristics of types. They enable compile-time type information inspection, such as whether a type is an integer, floating-point, an array, or if it supports certain operations. This information can be used to tailor template behavior to specific types, enhancing code robustness and flexibility.

Commonly Used Type Traits

- Type Categories: **std::is_integral<T>**, **std::is_floating_point<T>**, **std::is_array<T>**, etc., help determine the category of a type.
- Type Properties: **std::is_const<T>**, **std::is_volatile<T>**, and **std::is_pod<T>** (Plain Old Data) provide information about type properties.
- Type Relationships: std::is_same<T, U>, std::is_base_of<Base, Derived>, and std::is_convertible<From, To> enable checking relationships between types.
- Type Modifiers: **std::add_const<T>**, **std::remove_reference<T>**, etc., modify types in a generic way.

Using Type Traits in Templates

Type traits can significantly enhance template metaprogramming by enabling conditional compilation based on type characteristics. This allows for more generic, efficient, and error-free code.

Below is the sample program on Conditional Function Overloading based on Type Traits:

```
#include <iostream>
#include <type_traits>

template<typename T>
typename std::enable_if<std::is_integral<T>::value, T>::type
process(T value) {
 std::cout << "Processing integral type" << std::endl;
 return value + 1;
}

template<typename T>
typename std::enable_if<std::is_floating_point<T>::value, T>::type
process(T value) {
 std::cout << "Processing floating-point type" << std::endl;
 return value + 1.0;
}

int main() {
 std::cout << process(10) << std::endl; // Calls the integral version
 std::cout << process(3.14) << std::endl; // Calls the floating-point version
 return 0;
```

```
}
```

In the above given sample program, **std::enable_if** along with **std::is_integral** and **std::is_floating_point** type traits are used to select the appropriate function template overload based on the type of the argument. This pattern is a common use case of type traits for SFINAE.

Recipe 2: Use Custom Type Traits

Situation

Although there is a complete set of type traits provided by the C++ Standard Library, there are cases where more specific type behaviors or attributes need to be found. When this occurs, it is critical to define custom type traits. You can tailor C++'s type introspection capabilities to your needs with custom type traits, which improve the generalizability and robustness of template code and allow for more precise compile-time behavior customization.

Practical Solution

Defining Custom Type Traits

Creating a custom type trait involves defining a template structure that determines a particular characteristic of a type, typically by utilizing a combination of standard type traits, template specialization, and SFINAE.

Suppose our app requires serialization of various objects to a persistent storage or over a network. We want to differentiate between types that are serializable and those that are not, at compile time.

Below is the sample program on identifying serializable types:

```
#include <iostream>

#include <type_traits>



// Base template for is_serializable, defaults to false

template<typename T, typename = void>

struct is_serializable : std::false_type {};
```

```
// Specialization for types that have a serialize method
template<typename T>
struct is_serializable<T, std::void_t<decltype(std::declval<T>().serialize())>> :
std::true_type {};

// Usage example classes
class SerializableClass {
public:
 void serialize() const {
 std::cout << "Serializing SerializableClass" << std::endl;
 }
};

class NonSerializableClass {};

// Utility function to check serialization capability
template<typename T>
void serializeIfPossible(const T& obj) {
 if constexpr (is_serializable<T>::value) {
 obj.serialize();
 } else {
```

```
std::cout << "Type is not serializable" << std::endl;
}
}

int main() {
SerializableClass serializable;
NonSerializableClass nonSerializable;

serializeIfPossible(serializable); // This will call serialize
serializeIfPossible(nonSerializable); // This will print "Type is not serializable"
return 0;
}
```

In the above given sample program, **is_serializable** custom type trait checks for the existence of a **serialize** method within a type **T**. The specialization uses **std::void_t** and **decltype** to detect the presence of **serialize**, setting the trait to **true_type** if found. The utility function **serializeIfPossible** then uses this trait to conditionally compile code that serializes objects only if they are serializable. These traits facilitate a deeper understanding of type properties and behaviors, allowing for sophisticated compile-time logic that enhances the overall robustness and functionality of the application.

Recipe 3: Implement SFINAE Technique

Situation

Template code often needs to act differently depending on the types it operates on in certain scenarios. Nevertheless, not every type is capable of supporting every operation, and errors can occur when trying to compile unsupported operations. C++ template metaprogramming relies on the SFINAE principle, which enables the compiler to disregard specific template instantiations in the event of a substitution failure rather than interpreting it as a compilation error. Using this method, you can make templates that are more versatile and adaptable to different types.

Practical Solution

Understanding SFINAE

SFINAE is a rule in the C++ type system that allows for conditional compilation of code based on the success of type substitution in template functions. When a substitution leads to an invalid type or expression, it's not considered an error; instead, the compiler simply discards the template from the set of possible overloads or specializations.

Applying SFINAE with std::enable_if

One common way to apply SFINAE is by using **std::enable_if**, which conditionally enables or disables template specializations based on a compile-time boolean expression. This can be particularly useful for creating function overloads that are only available for certain types.

Suppose our application includes a utility function that should only apply to types that have an **iterate()** method, enabling iteration over elements of the type.

Given below is the sample example on conditional method specialization:

```
#include <iostream>

#include <type_traits>

#include <vector>


// Attempt to detect if T has an iterate() method

template<typename T, typename = std::void_t<>>

struct has_iterate : std::false_type {};


template<typename T>

struct has_iterate<T, std::void_t<decltype(std::declval<T>().iterate())>> : std::true_type
{};
```

```
// Utility function that only compiles if T has an iterate() method
template<typename T>
auto processElements(T& container) -> typename std::enable_if<has_iterate<T>::value,
void>::type {
 container.iterate([](const auto& element) {
 std::cout << element << std::endl;
 });
}

class IterableCollection {
public:
 void iterate(const std::function<void(int)>& func) {
 for (int element : {1, 2, 3}) {
 func(element);
 }
 }
};

int main() {
 IterableCollection myCollection;
 processElements(myCollection); // Compiles and runs
```

```
std::vector<int> myVector{1, 2, 3};

// processElements(myVector); // Won't compile: std::vector<int> does not have an iterate() method

return 0;

}
```

In the above given code snippet, the **has_iterate** type trait checks if a type **T** has an **iterate()** method. The **processElements** function template uses **std::enable_if** to ensure it's only available for types where **has_iterate<T>::value** is **true**. This leverages SFINAE to prevent compilation errors when attempting to use **processElements** with types lacking an **iterate()** method. By carefully applying SFINAE principles, such as with **std::enable_if** or through custom type traits, our application can include highly adaptable utilities and algorithms that maximize code reuse and maintainability.

Recipe 4: Implement Template Metaprogramming Technique

Situation

With the goal of improving performance, reducing runtime overhead, and guaranteeing type safety, our application attempts to fully utilize compile-time computation. With C++'s template metaprogramming (TMP) paradigm, code can be executed at compile time for a variety of purposes, including generic programming, calculations, type-based code generation, and decision-making. By handling complicated calculations and decisions during compilation, TMP can significantly improve and personalize applications.

Practical Solution

Understanding Template Metaprogramming

Template metaprogramming involves using C++ templates to produce metafunctions—templates that compute values or generate types and functions during compilation. TMP exploits the fact that the C++ template instantiation mechanism is Turing complete, meaning it can express any computation that a Turing machine can. This allows you to execute complex logic at compile time, leading to more efficient runtime code.

Key Concepts and Usage

- Compile-Time Computation: TMP can compute values at compile time, reducing runtime cost. For example, calculating factorial values or Fibonacci numbers for given constants.
- Type Manipulation: Generating types or selecting among types based on compile-time conditions, enhancing flexibility and type safety.
- Code Generation: Automatically generating customized code based on type traits or compile-time conditions, reducing boilerplate and manual specialization.

Following is the sample program on compile-time factorial calculation:

```
template<unsigned N>

struct Factorial {

 static constexpr unsigned value = N * Factorial<N - 1>::value;

};


template<>

struct Factorial<0> { // Base case specialization

 static constexpr unsigned value = 1;

};


int main() {

 constexpr unsigned result = Factorial<5>::value; // Computed at compile time

 static_assert(result == 120, "Factorial<5> should be 120");

 return 0;

}
```

The above sample program showcases a simple TMP application where a factorial is calculated at compile time. The **Factorial** template recursively defines **value** as **N** times the factorial of **N-1**, with a base case specialization for **Factorial<0>**. This results in **Factorial<5>::value** being computed during compilation.

Benefits for C++ Applications

- By performing computations at compile time, TMP can significantly reduce the runtime overhead, making applications faster and more responsive.
- TMP enables you to write more expressive type checks and operations, catching errors at compile time.
- Compile-time computations and decisions can lead to smaller and more efficient runtime code, as unnecessary branches or computations can be eliminated.

Opportunities for substantial optimizations and enhancements to code quality are presented by TMP's compile-time computations, type manipulations, and code generation. In high-performance computing, library development, and scenarios where compile-time computation is preferred or required, TMP's advantages in performance optimization, code customization, and type safety more than make up for the fact that it can make code more complicated and harder to understand.

Recipe 5: Using constexpr for Compile-Time Calculations

Situation

Some of the operations carried out by our application, like mathematical calculations or algorithmic decisions based on constant expressions, could be better handled at compile time. By introducing the constexpr specifier, C++ made it possible to do these kinds of evaluations at compile time, which significantly improved performance by cutting down on computations performed at runtime. For better and faster code execution, you can ensure that functions, objects, and variables are evaluated at compile time by declaring them as constexpr.

Practical Solution

Understanding constexpr

The **constexpr** specifier in C++ indicates that the value of a variable, the return value of a function, or the result of an object construction can be computed at compile time. This capability is crucial for enhancing application performance, especially in scenarios where certain values are known during compilation and don't change at runtime.

Usage of constexpr

constexpr Variables: Declaring variables as **constexpr** ensures their values are constant expressions and known at compile time.

constexpr Functions: Functions declared with **constexpr** are evaluated at compile time when given constant expressions as arguments. This is particularly useful for mathematical functions, utility functions, and constructors that initialize **constexpr** objects or values.

constexpr Constructors: Enables the creation of compile-time objects, useful for initializing constant data structures or performing compile-time calculations and validations.

Below is the sample program on Compile-Time prime number check wherein we are Implementing a compile-time function that checks if a number is prime:

```
constexpr bool isPrime(unsigned int number, unsigned int divisor = 2) {

 return (divisor * divisor > number) ? true :

 (number % divisor == 0) ? false : isPrime(number, divisor + 1);

}


int main() {

 static_assert(isPrime(5), "5 should be prime");

 static_assert(!isPrime(4), "4 should not be prime");


 constexpr bool primeResult = isPrime(11);

 std::cout << "Is 11 prime? " << (primeResult ? "Yes" : "No") << std::endl;


 return 0;

}
```

The above sample program demonstrates a **constexpr** function **isPrime** that calculates whether a number is prime at compile time. We use **static_assert** to check prime numbers during compilation, ensuring that these properties are verified without runtime overhead. Additionally, **constexpr** variables like **primeResult** can store results of compile-time calculations for runtime use.

Recipe 6: Advanced Use of decltype

Situation

To write code that is more generic and adaptable, it is crucial to use C++'s type deduction capabilities. The decltype keyword allows you to automatically adapt your templates and functions to the types of your inputs by evaluating the type of a specified expression at compile time. This is especially helpful when there is no explicit type specification but type preservation across complicated expressions is required, or when variables and templates are defined to match the type of an expression or function return type.

Practical Solution

Exploring decltype

decltype provides a way to extract the type from an expression, offering precise control over type deduction in templates and auto-typed variables. It becomes invaluable in template metaprogramming and situations where the type needs to be inferred without explicitly specifying it.

Usage Scenarios

- Type Matching: When defining variables that should match the type of an existing expression or variable.
- Perfect Forwarding: In combination with forwarding references, decltype can be used to perfectly forward arguments' types in template functions.
- Expression Return Type Deduction: For templated functions where the return type depends on the types of its parameters or their expressions.

Consider a function in our application that needs to perform operations on various types while preserving the input types' consistency through the operations.

```
#include <iostream>

#include <vector>
```

```
#include <type_traits>

template<typename T1, typename T2>
auto add(T1 a, T2 b) -> decltype(a + b) {
 return a + b;
}

template<typename Container, typename Index>
auto getElement(Container&& c, Index i) -> decltype(std::forward<Container>(c)[i]) {
 return std::forward<Container>(c)[i];
}

int main() {
 auto result = add(5, 4.3); // Uses decltype to deduce the return type as double
 static_assert(std::is_same<decltype(result), double>::value, "Result should be double");

 std::vector<int> vec = {1, 2, 3, 4, 5};
 auto elem = getElement(vec, 2); // Deduces return type as int&
 std::cout << "Element at index 2: " << elem << std::endl;

 return 0;
```

```
}
```

In these examples, **decltype** is used to deduce the return type of the **add** function based on its input types, allowing for type-safe arithmetic operations that preserve the correctness of the result type. Similarly, **getElement** utilizes **decltype** with forwarding references to deduce the return type as a reference or value depending on how the container is passed, ensuring type-consistent access to container elements.

Recipe 7: Implement Custom Compile-Time Functions

Situation

For modern applications to gracefully manage their compute-intensive features, efficient execution and optimization are essential at every level. Performance, accuracy, and efficiency are all enhanced by harnessing the power of compile-time computation. In order to minimize runtime overhead, C++ provides a number of methods to perform computations during compilation. Using constexpr and template metaprogramming techniques, you can create custom compile-time functions that execute logic, manipulate types, and do calculations before the program runs. This recipe delves into the design and implementation of these functions, making the most of C++'s compile-time capabilities for "GitforGits."

Practical Solution

Implementing Compile-Time Calculations with constexpr

constexpr functions are evaluated by the compiler when all their input arguments are known at compile time. Starting with C++11 and expanded in later standards, **constexpr** functions can contain a broader set of instructions, making them more powerful for compile-time logic.

Below is the sample program illustrating how to compile time power function:

```
constexpr int power(int base, int exp) noexcept {
 return (exp == 0) ? 1 : base * power(base, exp - 1);
}
```

```
static_assert(power(2, 5) == 32, "2 to the power of 5 should be 32");
```

This **constexpr** function calculates the power of a number in a recursive manner. Because it's **constexpr**, the computation is performed at compile time, and its correctness is verified with **static_assert**.

Template Metaprogramming for Type Manipulations

Template metaprogramming allows for more than just value computation; it can perform type manipulations and generate code based on types. This is particularly useful for creating generic libraries or frameworks that adapt to a wide variety of types.

Below is the sample program illustrating how to compile time type selection:

```
template<bool condition, typename TrueType, typename FalseType>

struct ConditionalType {

 using type = TrueType;

};


template<typename TrueType, typename FalseType>

struct ConditionalType<false, TrueType, FalseType> {

 using type = FalseType;

};


using ChosenType = ConditionalType<true, int, double>::type;

static_assert(std::is_same<ChosenType, int>::value, "ChosenType should be int");
```

This template structure **ConditionalType** acts similarly to the standard **std::conditional**, selecting one of two types based on a compile-time boolean condition. This kind of type manipulation is a core aspect of TMP, enabling highly flexible and reusable code structures.

Recipe 8: Implement Type Erasure Technique

Situation

Working with objects of unknown types while still performing type-specific operations is a must for applications operating in a highly dynamic environment. A versatile and type-safe method is therefore required to deal with this variety. To get around this problem and still maintain type safety and performance, C++ includes the Type Erasure technique, which abstracts away type details and allows operations on different types through a common interface. This method shines when designing APIs where the types of objects needed to complete specific interface contracts are unknown but can be held by container classes or when creating classes that can hold objects of any type.

Practical Solution

Understanding Type Erasure

Type Erasure is a pattern that decouples the specific type of an object from the way it is processed. It allows a system to use objects of different types interchangeably by focusing on the operations that can be performed on those objects rather than their concrete types. This is achieved by defining an interface that represents the operations and using polymorphism to handle the actual operations behind the scenes.

Implementing Type Erasure

The implementation typically involves a combination of interfaces (abstract base classes) and templates. The abstract base class defines the operations as virtual functions, while template classes provide concrete implementations that forward calls to the encapsulated object of any type.

Following is a simple program of Type Erasure used to create a type-agnostic container that can store and invoke a method on objects of any type:

```
#include <iostream>

#include <memory>



// The abstract base class representing any callable operation

class CallableBase {
```

```
public:
 virtual ~CallableBase() = default;
 virtual void call() const = 0;
};

// Template derived class for holding any callable entity
template<typename Func>
class Callable : public CallableBase {
 Func f;
public:
 Callable(Func f) : f(f) {}
 void call() const override {
 f();
 }
};

// Type-erased container for callable objects
class AnyCallable {
 std::unique_ptr<CallableBase> callable;
public:
 template<typename Func>
```

```
AnyCallable(Func f) : callable(new Callable<Func>(f)) {}

void call() const {
callable->call();
}
};

// Usage
int main() {
AnyCallable print([](){ std::cout << "Hello, Type Erasure!" << std::endl; });
print.call(); // Executes the lambda function

return 0;
}
```

The above sample program demonstrates a type-erased container, **AnyCallable**, that can store and invoke any callable entity. The key here is that the **AnyCallable** class does not need to know the type of the callable entity at compile time, enabling operations on various types through a common interface.

Benefits for C++ Applications

- Type Erasure allows for writing generic and flexible code that operates on a wide range of types.
- Unlike using **void*** or unions, Type Erasure provides a type-safe way to work with different types, as the operations allowed on the erased types are clearly defined through interfaces.

- It can offer performance benefits over other polymorphism techniques, such as dynamic polymorphism, by minimizing overhead in certain scenarios.

Type Erasure facilitates writing reusable, maintainable, and efficient code that can adapt to different types dynamically. This technique is especially valuable in library design, plugin architectures, and systems where operations on diverse object types are required.

Summary

This chapter presented an in-depth tour of C++'s type system and demonstrated methods that allow programmers to create code that is more expressive, efficient, and type-safe. Beginning with type traits and utilities, the chapter laid the groundwork for compile-time type introspection and manipulation, allowing the development of generic code that can adapt to a wide range of types. The investigation of custom type traits expanded on this capability, allowing for the creation of application-specific traits that cater to specific requirements, thereby increasing template metaprogramming's power and versatility.

The chapter through advanced type manipulation techniques revealed the utility of SFINAE in creating robust templates that gracefully handle type variability. The chapter then moved on to template metaprogramming, which demonstrated how to perform complex compile-time computations and type manipulations, resulting in more optimized and scalable applications. The introduction of constexpr for compile-time calculations provided opportunities for performance optimization, while the advanced use of decltype enabled precise type deduction in complex scenarios. Implementing custom compile-time functions demonstrated the power of compile-time execution in ensuring program accuracy and efficiency. Finally, Type Erasure was investigated, presenting a sophisticated method for achieving runtime type flexibility without sacrificing type safety, completing the toolkit for advanced type manipulation in C++ applications. This chapter not only demonstrated the depth and power of C++'s type system, but also provided you with the knowledge to use these features to create highly generic, efficient, and maintainable code.

CHAPTER 10: FILE I/O AND STREAMS OPERATIONS

Introduction

An essential part of programming that interacts with external data sources and sinks is learning how to handle file input/output (I/O) and stream operations in C++. This chapter starts on that path. This chapter is designed to provide you with the skills you need to read and write files, modify data streams, and handle I/O operations with delicacy. It seeks to adapt to the different needs of the GitforGits app.

In Performing Basic File Operations, we lay the groundwork for more advanced I/O operations by covering the fundamentals of reading and writing files. Among the tasks covered include reading file contents into variables, writing data back to Text and Binary files, and comparing and contrasting the two formats along with the best practices for each. Next, we will examine Using Stream Buffers in detail to directly interact with a stream's underlying buffer, allowing for more controlled and efficient data processing, as we move on to Optimizing I/O Operations for Performance and Reliability in Manipulating Efficient File Streams.

After establishing thorough procedures for checking for errors and handling exceptions, the chapter moves on to learn how to handle file errors and manage exceptions during file operations. Data readability and usability are improved using the techniques introduced in Advanced Stream Manipulators and Formatting, which allow precise control over output formatting and input parsing. We investigate ways to define custom behavior for stream buffers and expand the standard library's I/O capabilities in Implementing Custom Streambuf Classes.

The global aspect of modern software is further emphasized by Stream Locales and Facets for Internationalization, which train you to build programs that support different languages and regional settings. Finally, as a valuable tool for situations where data doesn't need to be saved externally, Memory Streams for Efficient Data Processing addresses employing streams for in-memory data manipulation. Chapter 10 offers a thorough introduction to C++ file I/O and stream operations through these recipes, allowing you to create more powerful, efficient, and globally accessible programs.

Recipe 1: Perform Basic File Operations: Reading and Writing

Situation

A standard need of many applications is the ability to read and write files. Processing user-generated content, configuration management, data persistence, or logging all require efficient and accurate handling of file operations. The application's functionality and user experience are enhanced by its ability to perform these activities smoothly interact with the filesystem.

Practical Solution

Opening a File

The first step in file I/O in C++ involves opening the file using an **fstream**, **ifstream**, or **ofstream** object for reading, writing, or both. The file mode (e.g., read, write, append) is specified at the time of opening.

```
#include <fstream>

#include <iostream>

#include <string>


void writeToFile(const std::string& filename, const std::string& content) {

 std::ofstream file(filename);

 if (!file.is_open()) {

 std::cerr << "Failed to open " << filename << '\n';

 return;

 }

 file << content;

}


std::string readFromFile(const std::string& filename) {

 std::ifstream file(filename);

 std::string content, line;

 while (getline(file, line)) {
```

```
content += line + '\n';
}
return content;
}
```

Writing to a File

After opening the file in write mode (using **std::ofstream**), data can be written to the file using the insertion operator (**<<**). Always check that the file has been successfully opened before attempting to write to it.

Reading from a File

To read from a file, open it in read mode (using **std::ifstream**) and use the extraction operator (**>>**) for formatted input or **std::getline()** for reading lines. Loop until all data is read, typically checking the stream's state to ensure successful reads.

Handling File Errors and Exceptions

Error handling is an integral part of file I/O operations. Checking the stream's state (e.g., **file.is_open()**, **file.fail()**) helps identify issues like failure to open a file or read/write errors. C++ streams can also be set to throw exceptions on failures by using **file.exceptions(std::ifstream::failbit | std::ifstream::badbit)**.

Basic file operations are a common feature of C++ programming, allowing GitforGits to interface with the file system successfully. These actions lay the groundwork for more complicated file handling and data processing duties, ensuring that programs manage their data efficiently and reliably.

Recipe 2: Work with Text and Binary Files

Situation

GitforGits maintains a variety of data types, including user-generated content, application settings, and logs. Depending on the type of data, it can be stored in either text or binary format. Text files are human-readable and easier to edit and debug, whereas binary files are more efficient in terms of storage and speed, especially for numerical data or serialised objects. Understanding how to operate with both file types is critical for improving the application's storage, performance, and compatibility.

Practical Solution

Text Files

- Reading and Writing: Utilize **std::ifstream** and **std::ofstream** with the default mode. Text files are accessed line by line or as formatted data using operators **>>** and **<<**.
- Advantages: Ease of use, human-readable and editable with standard text editors, and simplified parsing of structured data (like CSV).
- Usage Example: Logging events or user actions, configuration files.

```
void writeToTextFile(const std::string& filename, const std::string& content) {
 std::ofstream file(filename);
 file << content;
}


std::string readFromTextFile(const std::string& filename) {
 std::ifstream file(filename);
 std::string content((std::istreambuf_iterator<char>(file)),
std::istreambuf_iterator<char>());
 return content;
}
```

Binary Files

- Reading and Writing: Open files with **std::ios::binary** flag in addition to **std::ifstream** or **std::ofstream** to ensure data is read/written in binary form. Use **read** and **write** member functions for unformatted data transfer.
- Advantages: More compact storage, faster read/write operations due to lack of encoding/decoding, and direct mapping to in-memory data structures.
- Usage Example: Storing complex data structures, images, or encrypted data.

```
void writeToBinaryFile(const std::string& filename, const std::vector<int>& data) {
 std::ofstream file(filename, std::ios::binary);
 file.write(reinterpret_cast<const char*>(data.data()), data.size() * sizeof(int));
}

std::vector<int> readFromBinaryFile(const std::string& filename) {
 std::ifstream file(filename, std::ios::binary);
 std::vector<int> data((std::istreambuf_iterator<char>(file)),
std::istreambuf_iterator<char>());
 return data;
}
```

Efficient processing of text and binary files in GitforGits necessitates a thorough awareness of the merits and drawbacks of each type. While text files are simple and easy to read for basic data storage and configuration tasks, binary files excel in terms of performance and efficiency for storing complicated or large amounts of data.

Recipe 3: Manipulate Efficient File Streams

Situation

Given that GitforGits handles a large quantity of data, it requires not just the ability to read from and write to files, but also the ability to do so efficiently. Handling file streams correctly can significantly improve speed, especially when working with huge files or when I/O activities become a bottleneck. Optimizing file stream manipulation entails knowing buffer management, stream placement, and other approaches for reducing overhead and increasing data processing performance.

Practical Solution

Buffer Management

File streams in C++ use buffers to minimize direct disk I/O operations, which are costly in terms of performance. By managing the buffer effectively, you can enhance the efficiency of file operations. Adjusting the buffer size used by a file stream can optimize performance based on the nature of the data and the system's characteristics. Larger buffers might improve performance for sequential file access by reducing the number of I/O operations.

```
#include <fstream>

char customBuffer[8192]; // Define a custom buffer size



std::ofstream outputFile("example.dat", std::ios::binary);

outputFile.rdbuf()->pubsetbuf(customBuffer, sizeof(customBuffer));
```

Stream Positioning

Navigating efficiently within a file stream is crucial for random access file operations. Utilizing seek operations (**seekg** for **ifstream**, **seekp** for **ofstream**) allows you to jump to different positions within a file, enabling efficient reading and writing from/to specific locations. For large files, seek operations must be used judiciously to avoid unnecessary positioning that could lead to performance degradation.

```
std::ifstream inputFile("largeFile.dat", std::ios::binary);

inputFile.seekg(1000, std::ios::beg); // Move to the 1001st byte in the file
```

Efficiently Reading and Writing

Repeatedly using the extraction (**>>**) and insertion (**<<**) operators can be less efficient than reading or writing larger blocks of data at once, especially for binary files.

```
std::vector<char> buffer(1024);

inputFile.read(buffer.data(), buffer.size()); // Read 1024 bytes into buffer

outputFile.write(buffer.data(), buffer.size()); // Write buffer to file
```

Managing Stream State and Errors

Properly managing the stream state (e.g., EOF, fail, and bad bits) and clearing errors when necessary ensures that file streams continue to operate smoothly even after encountering issues. After a failed operation or when reusing streams, resetting the stream state allows further operations to proceed.

```
if (!inputFile.eof()) {

 inputFile.clear(); // Clear error flags

 inputFile.seekg(0, std::ios::beg); // Rewind the stream for another operation

}
```

Efficient manipulation of file streams is critical for programs that handle large amounts of data. "GitforGits" can enhance file I/O speed significantly by optimizing buffer utilization, using intelligent stream positioning, and properly managing stream state. The program may load, process, and store data more efficiently with the help of these techniques, which improve system responsiveness and throughput. High-performance file handling is built upon them.

Recipe 4: Use Stream Buffers

Situation

Direct interaction with stream buffers is necessary for our application to achieve even higher levels of control and performance, in addition to efficient file I/O operations. When working with files, standard input/output, or even in-memory storage, file streams (std::ifstream, std::ofstream) in C++ rely on stream buffers as their foundational mechanism. By eliminating unnecessary steps and providing finer-grained control over input/output operations, stream buffers can significantly improve data processing efficiency.

Practical Solution

Understanding Stream Buffers

A stream buffer, represented by **std::streambuf**, is the component that actually handles the storage, management, and transfer of data between the program and the external device or memory. Working directly with stream buffers bypasses some of the higher-level stream functionalities, providing lower-level, more efficient access to the data.

Basic Operations with Stream Buffers

Directly interacting with the buffer can be more efficient for certain operations, as it allows bypassing the formatting and state checking mechanisms of the streams.

Following is how to use stream buffers for efficiently copying data from one file to another without unnecessary formatting overhead:

```
#include <fstream>

#include <iostream>


void copyFileUsingStreamBuffers(const std::string& sourcePath, const std::string&
destinationPath) {

 std::ifstream source(sourcePath, std::ios::binary);

 std::ofstream destination(destinationPath, std::ios::binary);


 if (!source.is_open() || !destination.is_open()) {

 std::cerr << "Error opening files." << std::endl;

 return;

 }


 // Obtain the stream buffer of the source file

 std::streambuf* sourceBuf = source.rdbuf();


 // Use the stream buffer directly to copy data to the destination file

 destination << sourceBuf;
```

```
// Both streams are automatically closed when going out of scope
}

int main() {
 copyFileUsingStreamBuffers("source.dat", "destination.dat");
 return 0;
}
```

In the above given sample program, the stream buffer of the source file is directly used to copy its contents to the destination file. This method is particularly effective for large binary file transfers, where formatting and type conversions are unnecessary. A direct route to high-performance data processing in C++ programs is to use stream buffers. It allows for low-level, efficient access to I/O operations, which gives you the freedom to tweak or optimize the way file streams work. Learning about and making use of stream buffers can significantly improve an application's data processing efficiency, whether for basic data transfer tasks or more advanced custom buffer manipulations.

Recipe 5: Handle File Errors

Situation

Because errors can occur for a variety of reasons (e.g., due to disk space limitations, permissions issues, or the file not existing), it is critical to handle file I/O operations carefully while working on app development. The application's continued dependability and user-friendliness are guaranteed by its robust file error handling, which promptly addresses problems by giving clear feedback and implementing suitable actions. When dealing with file operations, it's important to do more than simply catch exceptions; you should also look for possible errors ahead of time and react appropriately to them.

Practical Solution

Error Handling Strategies

- Preemptive Checks: Before attempting file operations, perform checks to ensure the operation is likely to succeed. This includes checking if the file exists, if there is enough disk space, or if the application has the necessary permissions.
- Stream State Checking: After each file I/O operation, check the stream's state using methods like **good()**, **eof()**, **fail()**, and **bad()**. These checks help determine the outcome of the operation and take necessary corrective actions.

Following is the sample program on safe file reading:

```
#include <fstream>

#include <iostream>

#include <vector>


bool safeFileRead(const std::string& filePath, std::vector<char>& buffer) {

 std::ifstream file(filePath, std::ios::binary);


 // Check if the file stream successfully opened

 if (!file) {

 std::cerr << "Error opening file: " << filePath << std::endl;

 return false;

 }


 // Attempt to read the file contents into the buffer

 file.seekg(0, std::ios::end);

 size_t fileSize = file.tellg();

 file.seekg(0, std::ios::beg);
```

```
buffer.resize(fileSize);

if (!file.read(buffer.data(), fileSize)) {

std::cerr << "Error reading file: " << filePath << std::endl;

return false;

}


return true; // Indicate success

}
```

In the above given sample program, the code safely attempts to read a file into a buffer. It checks whether the file stream is open before reading and verifies if the entire file has been successfully read. These checks help prevent errors from going unnoticed and allow for appropriate error handling or messaging to the user.

Modern C++ I/O operations can throw exceptions. Using **try-catch** blocks around file operations can catch and handle these exceptions gracefully.

Following is the sample program on exception handling in file operations:

```
void writeFileWithExceptionHandling(const std::string& filePath, const std::string&
content) {

std::ofstream file;

try {

file.exceptions(std::ofstream::failbit | std::ofstream::badbit);

file.open(filePath);

file << content;

} catch (const std::ofstream::failure& e) {

std::cerr << "Exception occurred: " << e.what() << std::endl;
```

```
}
}
```

This function demonstrates how to enable exceptions for **std::ofstream** and use **try-catch** to handle any errors that occur during file opening or writing. Enabling exceptions for stream operations provides a clear mechanism to handle errors directly associated with those operations.

Recipe 6: Manage Exceptions

Situation

Finally, strong exception handling is critical, particularly for file I/O operations that can encounter runtime errors like file not found, permission denied, or disk full. By handling errors gracefully and giving useful feedback to the user or logs, effective exception management guarantees the application's stability. Methods for handling exceptions in C++ file I/O operations are covered in this recipe, with an emphasis on controlled methods for catching, processing, and recovering from them.

Practical Solution

Understanding C++ Exceptions for File I/O

C++ uses exceptions to signal errors that occur at runtime. The standard library (including I/O operations) throws exceptions to indicate failure conditions. Properly managing these exceptions allows a program to react to error conditions without crashing or entering an undefined state.

Key Strategies for Exception Management

By default, C++ stream objects do not throw exceptions for I/O operations. Enabling exceptions for streams is critical to catching errors effectively.

```
std::ifstream file;
file.exceptions(std::ifstream::badbit | std::ifstream::failbit);
```

Use **try-catch** blocks around file operations to catch exceptions. It's important to catch exceptions by const reference (**const std::exception&**) to avoid slicing and to handle all possible exception types correctly.

```
try {
 std::ifstream file("nonexistent_file.txt");
 // Use the file here
} catch (const std::ifstream::failure& e) {
 std::cerr << "Exception opening/reading file: " << e.what() << '\n';
} catch (const std::exception& e) {
 std::cerr << "Standard exception: " << e.what() << '\n';
} catch (...) {
 std::cerr << "Unknown exception occurred" << '\n';
}
```

Custom Exception Classes

For application-specific errors, defining custom exception classes derived from **std::exception** allows for more descriptive error handling.

```
class FileError : public std::exception {
 std::string message;
public:
 explicit FileError(const std::string& msg) : message(msg) {}
 const char* what() const noexcept override {
 return message.c_str();
 }
};
```

Using custom exceptions enables your application to handle errors more appropriately and provide clearer messages to the user or system logs. By enabling exceptions for stream operations, utilizing **try-catch** blocks to catch and handle exceptions, and adhering to exception safety guarantees, you can safeguard against potential runtime errors.

Recipe 7: Advanced Stream Manipulators and Formatting

Situation

Extensive control over output formatting is necessary for any app that requires precise data handling, presentation, and logging. You can customize the presentation of data streams with the help of the C++ Standard Library's extensive stream manipulators and formatting options. The application's output clarity and user interface can be significantly improved by learning and using advanced stream manipulators. These tools are useful for aligning text, formatting numerical data, and managing the precision of floating-point representations.

Practical Solution

Leveraging Stream Manipulators

Stream manipulators are special functions or objects in C++ that modify the state of streams. They can be used to alter how data is read from or written to streams, providing control over formatting, alignment, fill characters, and numeric bases, among other aspects.

Formatting Output

- Fixed and Scientific Notation: Use **std::fixed** and **std::scientific** to control the formatting of floating-point values.
- Set Precision: **std::setprecision(int n)** determines the number of digits displayed for floating-point values.
- Width and Fill: Control field width with **std::setw(int n)** and fill characters with **std::setfill(char c)** for aligning output.

```
#include <iostream>

#include <iomanip>

#include <vector>
```

```
void displayData(const std::vector<double>& data) {
 std::cout << std::fixed << std::setprecision(2);
 for (const auto& value : data) {
 std::cout << "Value: " << std::setw(10) << std::setfill('*') << value << '\n';
 }
}
```

Manipulating Numeric Bases and Booleans

- Hexadecimal, Octal, and Decimal: **std::hex**, **std::oct**, and **std::dec** switch the numeric base for integer I/O.
- Boolean Formatting: **std::boolalpha** and **std::noboolalpha** toggle between textual (**true**/**false**) and numeric (**1**/**0**) representations of booleans.

```
std::cout << std::boolalpha << true << " or " << std::noboolalpha << true << '\n';
std::cout << std::hex << 255 << " in hex is " << std::dec << 255 << " in decimal\n";
```

Custom Manipulators

Developing custom stream manipulators involves creating functions or function templates that take stream objects as arguments and modify their state or perform specific operations.

Below is the sample program on custom indent manipulator:

```
#include <iostream>
#include <sstream>


class Indenter {
 int level;
```

```
public:
 explicit Indenter(int level) : level(level) {}
 friend std::ostream& operator<<(std::ostream& os, const Indenter& indent) {
 for (int i = 0; i < indent.level; ++i) os.put(' ');
 return os;
 }
};

// Usage
std::cout << Indenter(4) << "Indented Text\n";
```

The above sample program showcases how to create a custom manipulator **Indenter** that adds indentation to the output, enhancing readability, especially for hierarchical or structured data.

All of the aforementioned sophisticated C++ stream manipulators and formatting tools allow programmers to generate code that is both easy to read and organize. Using these features, our application can improve the user experience and make debugging easier by providing a more polished UI and clearer logging. These advantages are taken to the next level with custom manipulators, which enable output customization according to application needs, thus improving the program's interaction with users and other systems in terms of both quality and utility.

Recipe 8: Implement Custom Streambuf Classes

Situation

Sometimes, the application's requirements may differ from what the standard stream buffer capabilities offered by C++ can handle. This could be because the application needs to log in a different format, buffer data in a different way, or integrate with non-standard external data sources. The required adaptability and command can be achieved in such situations by incorporating custom stream buffer (streambuf) classes. To make streams behave exactly as needed by applications, you can modify the way data is read or written to streams by intercepting stream operations with a custom streambuf.

Practical Solution

Basics of Custom Streambuf Implementation

A custom **streambuf** class derives from **std::streambuf** and overrides its virtual functions to manage the stream's buffer. Key functions include **overflow()**, **underflow()**, and **sync()**, which handle writing to the buffer, reading from the buffer, and flushing the buffer, respectively.

Creating a Custom Output Streambuf

The **overflow(int ch)** method is crucial for custom output stream buffers. It's called when the buffer is full or when a character needs to be written directly. Given below is how to implement a simple custom streambuf that redirects output to both the console and a file:

```
#include <streambuf>

#include <iostream>

#include <fstream>


class DualStreamBuf : public std::streambuf {

 std::ostream& stream1;

 std::ostream& stream2;

protected:

 // Override overflow to write characters to both streams

 int overflow(int c) override {

 if (c != EOF) {

 stream1.put(c);

 stream2.put(c);
```

```
 stream1.flush();

 stream2.flush();

 }

 return c;

 }

public:

 DualStreamBuf(std::ostream& s1, std::ostream& s2) : stream1(s1), stream2(s2) {}

};

// Usage example

int main() {

 std::ofstream file("log.txt");

 DualStreamBuf dualBuf(std::cout, file);

 std::ostream dualStream(&dualBuf);

 dualStream << "Message logged to console and file\n";

 return 0;

}
```

This **DualStreamBuf** class directs output to two different **ostream** objects, allowing simultaneous logging to the console and a file. By overriding **overflow()**, it ensures that each character written to the stream is sent to both destinations.

Custom Input Streambuf

Implementing a custom input stream buffer involves overriding the **underflow()** method, which refills the buffer when it's exhausted. This is particularly useful for parsing or preprocessing input data on-the-fly.

Following are the benefits:

- Performance: Custom stream buffers can be optimized for specific use cases, potentially offering performance improvements over generic implementations.
- Flexibility: They provide unparalleled control over input/output operations, allowing for innovative solutions to complex I/O requirements.
- Integration: Custom **streambuf** classes can integrate C++ streams with external systems or libraries not originally designed for C++ stream operations.

Recipe 9: Stream Locales and Facets for Internationalization

Situation

In order to accommodate users from all over the world, our application will need to be able to work with a variety of languages and cultural norms. It is essential to handle data and text that is formatted according to different regional standards, such as different representations of numbers, different character encodings, and date formats. C++ streams provide a complex method of localization and facet-based internationalization. Specific cultural conventions are represented by locales, and behaviors for formatting and parsing data types according to those conventions are defined by facets. When used correctly, they can significantly improve the app's usability in various regions.

Practical Solution

Understanding Locales and Facets

A locale in C++ is an object that encapsulates cultural-specific information. Facets are parts of a locale that handle specific localization tasks, such as formatting numbers, currency, dates, and times, or converting between uppercase and lowercase in a way that respects local rules.

Setting Stream Locale

To handle internationalized input and output, you can set the locale of a stream. This affects how the stream interprets input and formats output.

```
#include <iostream>
#include <locale>

void setupStreamLocale() {
 // Set the global locale to the system default
 std::locale::global(std::locale(""));

 // Apply the global locale to standard output stream
 std::cout.imbue(std::locale());

 std::cout << 123456.78 << "\n"; // Output format may vary based on system locale
}
```

Using Locale Facets for Formatting

You can use specific facets of a locale to format data according to regional conventions. The **std::num_put** and **std::num_get** facets, for example, are used for output and input of numbers.

```
#include <iomanip>

void formatWithLocale() {
 std::locale myLocale(""); // Create a locale based on the user's environment
 std::cout.imbue(myLocale); // Set the locale for cout
```

```
// Use std::put_money for currency formatting according to locale

std::cout << std::showbase << std::put_money(123456) << std::endl;

}
```

Custom Locales for Internationalization

Beyond using the system's locales, C++ allows the creation of custom locales that can be used to tailor behavior for specific internationalization needs. This can be particularly useful for applications that need to support locales not directly available on the user's system.

```
#include <sstream>

#include <locale>


void useCustomLocale() {

// Create a custom locale based on the current locale but with a different thousands separator

std::locale customLocale(std::locale(), new std::numpunct<char>{

','

});


std::stringstream ss;

ss.imbue(customLocale);

ss << std::fixed << std::setprecision(2) << 1000000.00;


std::cout << ss.str() << std::endl; // "1,000,000.00" with custom thousands separator
```

```
}
```

A strong foundation for internationalization can be found in locales and facets, which allow for the formatting of dates and numbers according to local standards and the display of text in the correct language and encoding. Applications that intend to reach users all over the world must have this capability so that they can accommodate the wide range of cultural norms that your users may have.

Recipe 10: Memory Streams for Efficient Data Processing

Situation

Some of the data processed by "GitforGits"—such as intermediate processing results, data buffering, or temporary storage for serialization—does not require immediate or even delayed persistence to disk. Reading and writing to disk might become excessively sluggish and resource-intensive under these conditions. A solution for efficient and fast data processing is memory streams, which execute I/O operations in memory. Using memory streams can significantly improve application performance by speeding up these operations and removing the need to access the disk.

Practical Solution

Understanding Memory Streams

C++ provides memory stream classes through **std::stringstream**, **std::istringstream**, and **std::ostringstream** that work with **std::string** buffers. These streams offer the same interface as file and console I/O streams but operate on strings in memory. This makes them ideal for tasks requiring fast I/O operations without actual file access, such as parsing, formatting, and temporary data storage.

Using std::stringstream for Data Manipulation

std::stringstream is a versatile memory stream class capable of both input and output operations. It can be used to construct strings from mixed data types or parse strings into various types.

```
#include <sstream>

#include <iostream>
```

```
void demonstrateStringStream() {
 std::stringstream ss;

 // Output to stringstream
 ss << "Date: " << 2024 << "-" << 3 << "-" << 15;
 std::string dateStr = ss.str(); // Retrieve the constructed string
 std::cout << dateStr << std::endl;

 // Clear the stream and reuse for input
 ss.str("123 456");
 ss.clear(); // Clear state flags

 int num1, num2;
 ss >> num1 >> num2;
 std::cout << "Parsed numbers: " << num1 << ", " << num2 << std::endl;
}
```

std::istringstream and std::ostringstream for Specific Tasks

While **std::stringstream** handles both input and output, **std::istringstream** and **std::ostringstream** are specialized for input and output operations, respectively. Use **std::istringstream** for parsing strings and **std::ostringstream** for efficiently composing strings.

```
void parseString(const std::string& input) {
```

```
std::istringstream iss(input);

int year, month, day;

char dash1, dash2;

if (!(iss >> year >> dash1 >> month >> dash2 >> day) || dash1 != '-' || dash2 != '-')
{

std::cerr << "Parsing failed." << std::endl;

return;

}

std::cout << "Parsed date: " << year << "-" << month << "-" << day << std::endl;

}
```

Without the overhead of disk access, the application can execute complex parsing, formatting, and temporary data storage by utilizing std::stringstream, std::istringstream, and std::ostringstream. Applications that necessitate quick data transformations or manipulations benefit significantly from this method, which enhances performance and responsiveness.

Summary

With the knowledge we gained in this chapter, we will be able to navigate the complex world of C++ stream manipulation and file handling with ease in "GitforGits." Beginning with the basics of file reading and writing, the chapter established a firm groundwork for learning how to work with text and binary files, stressing the significance of learning the ins and outs of each format for efficient data processing. The importance of buffer management and stream positioning in improving performance was brought to light as we dove deeper into the topic of stream buffers and file stream manipulation, which shed light on advanced techniques for optimizing I/O operations.

A strong foundation for developing resilient apps that can recover gracefully from unforeseen situations was laid out by additional research into handling file errors and managing exceptions. The chapter also covered advanced stream manipulators and formatting, which are crucial for making readable logs and user-friendly interfaces because they give you exact control over how the output looks and how the data is interpreted. C++ streams' power and adaptability were on full display with the introduction of custom streambuf classes, which allowed for new ways to modify stream behavior to meet particular needs. In addition, our application can accommodate a wide range of users because it incorporates locales and internationalization features, which solve the problems associated with developing global applications. At last, memory streams were a game-changer in terms of data efficiency; they allowed for operations to run at high speeds without the delay that comes with accessing disks. Along with providing you with the tools to better handle data, this comprehensive chapter through file I/O and streams has also highlighted the importance of precision, efficiency, and adaptability in managing data, which is the lifeblood of any application.

Index

T

V

Epilogue

Looking back on the chapters we've learned together through the vastness of C++ programming, I can't help but feel a sense of accomplishment as we near the end. With all these chapters coming to a conclusion, I hope that this book has been a trustworthy instruction, shedding light on the particulars of C++ and the technical aspects of software development, for those who are trying to make their way through the complexity of modern C++.

In this book, we have covered a lot of ground, from the basics of C++11/17/20/23 to the complex methods used in high-performance applications. Throughout all these chapters, I attempted to arm you with more than just the technical skills necessary to develop code. I want you to be able to analyze problems critically, apply solutions efficiently, and understand why particular approaches are used. The belief that becoming an expert in C++ is an ongoing process of discovery and learning should be your takeaway from this book, if nothing else.

Fundamentally, programming is an artistic profession. Our knowledge, our goals, and our desire to create something significant are all reflected in every line of code we write. The difficulties we face are not roadblocks but rather chances to learn, improve, and reach new heights of understanding. The purpose of sharing these anecdotes is to draw from my personal experiences; I hope that they speak to you, motivate you, and inspire you to keep going when the going gets tough.

The future of C++ and the software development industry is filled with endless change. We will be able to do more with code in the future because new standards will appear, bringing new capabilities and paradigms. Keep an open mind, try new things, and be active in the C++ development community; I hope you'll do all three. The growth of this ecosystem is dependent on your contributions—discussions, code, and initiatives.

With that said, I want to express my deepest appreciation for coming along on this tricky, messy but solvable challenges with me. There are many twists and turns on the path to mastery, but there are also many chances for development, experimentation, and new knowledge. I hope that you find this guide helpful as you delve deeper into the exciting and expansive realm of C++ programming. Never stop learning new things, never stop coding, and most importantly, never stop sharing what you know with the world. Each of us makes a difference in shaping technology's future, and I can't wait to see the amazing things you make.

Thank You

www.ingramcontent.com/pod-product-compliance
Lightning Source LLC
Chambersburg PA
CBHW080211170726
48282CB00030B/1075
9788119177622